foll quilt appliqué

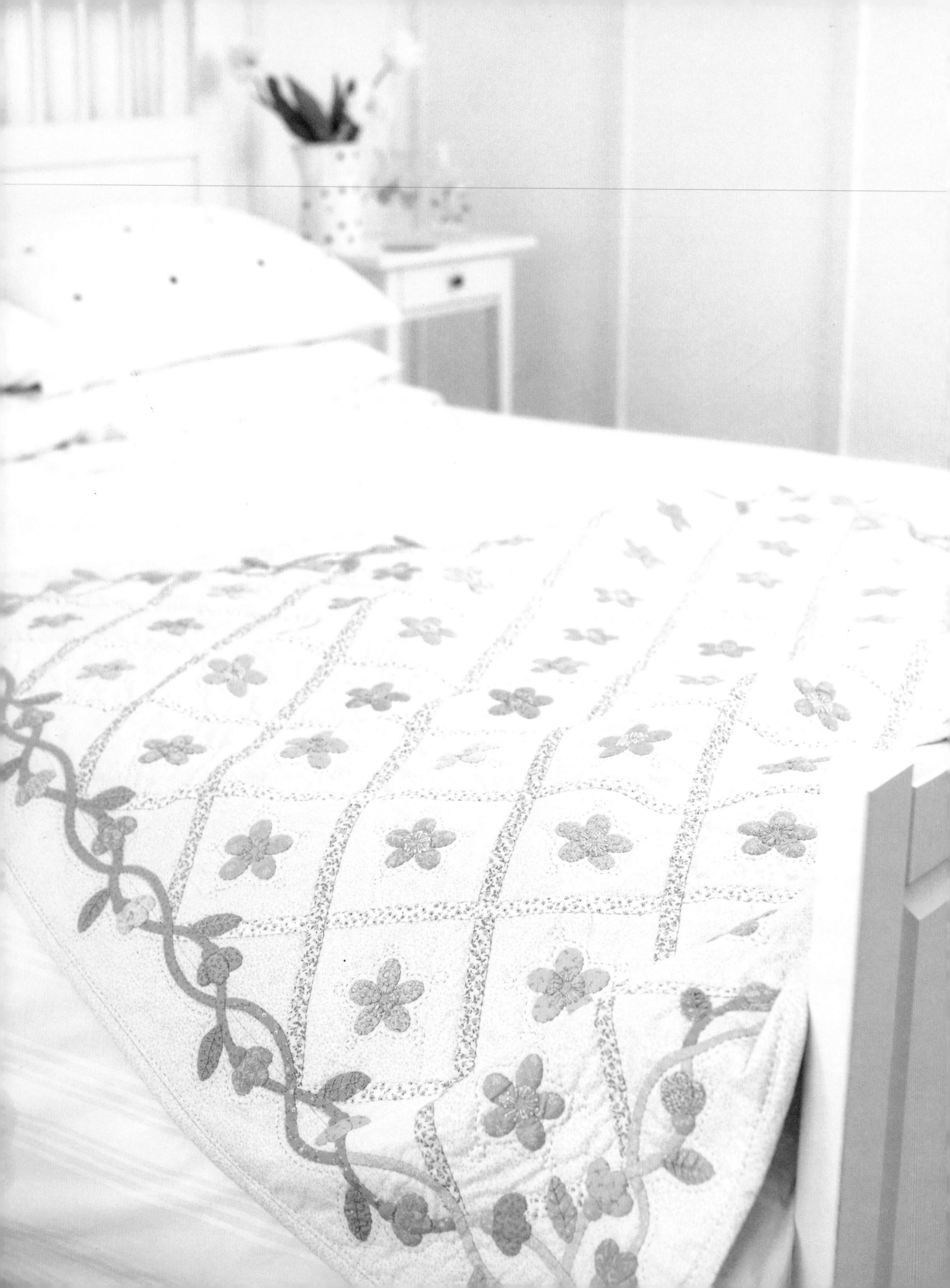

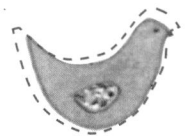

folk quilt appliqué

IRRESISTIBLE PROJECTS, CLEVER TECHNIQUES

Clare Kingslake

D&C
David and Charles
www.rucraft.co.uk

This book is dedicated to my dearest sister Jane, for her love and support and our fun together at quilt shows. To my children Jonny, Lottie and step-son Jack, for their patience when I talk endlessly about quilts. For my husband Peter, for his love and support, not minding about threads all over the floor and doing a lot of the cooking. To my dearest dad, John, for being DAD, and to the memory of my Mum, Miriam Cannon, who taught me to sew and to look at the beauty of the land.

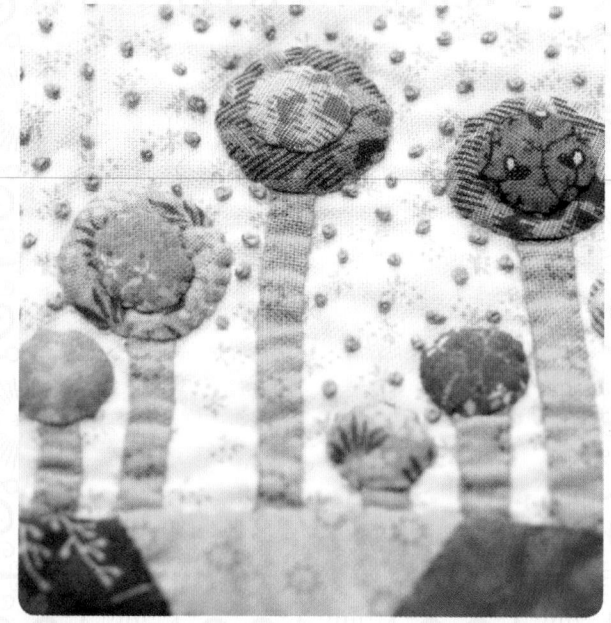

A DAVID & CHARLES BOOK
© F&W Media International, LTD 2011

David & Charles is an imprint of F&W Media International, LTD
Brunel House, Forde Close, Newton Abbot, TQ12 4PU, UK

F&W Media International, LTD is a subsidiary of F+W Media Inc.
4700 East Galbraith Road, Cincinnati, OH 45236, USA

First published in the UK and USA in 2011

Text and designs © Clare Kingslake 2011
Layout and photography © F&W Media International, LTD 2011

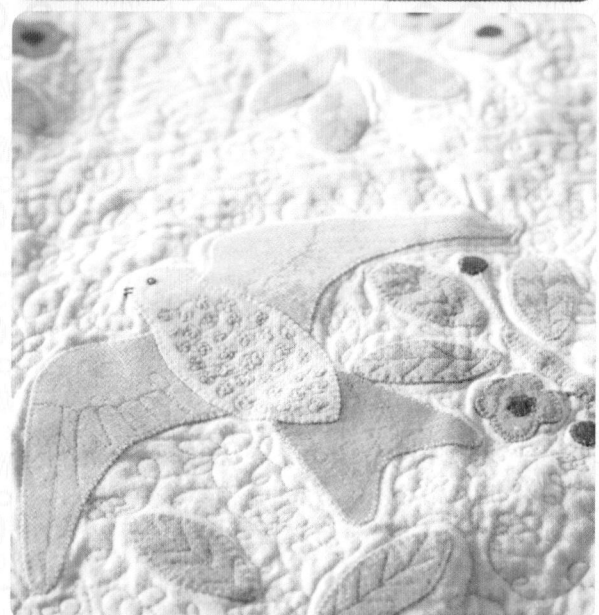

ISBN-13: 978-0-7153-3826-1 paperback
ISBN-10: 0-7153-3826-9 paperback

Printed in China by RR Donnelley
for F&W Media International, LTD
Brunel House, Forde Close, Newton Abbot, TQ12 4PU, UK

Publisher Alison Myer
Acquisitions Editor Cheryl Brown
Assistant Editor Jeni Hennah
Project Editor Lin Clements
Design Manager Sarah Clark
Illustrator Mia Trenoweth
Photographer Sian Irvine
Senior Production Controller Kelly Smith

F+W Media Inc. publishes high quality books on a wide range of subjects. For more great book ideas visit: **www.rucraft.co.uk**

Contents

Introduction 6
Fabric Selection 8

Drying in the Breeze 10
Christmas Angel 18
Woven Baskets 28
Under the Greenwood Tree 40
Daisy Table Setting 46
Lollipop Flowers 56
Rose Bouquet 66
Birds of a Feather 74
Buttercup, Buttercup 82

Tools and Equipment 94
Techniques 96
Templates 110

Acknowledgments 127
Suppliers 127
About the Author 127
Index 128

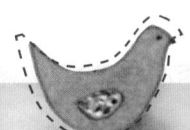

Introduction

As I look out of the window on to the garden and see how the sunlight casts shadows on the plants I marvel at the different colours, shapes, subtleties and harmony. Rustic scenes such as these inspire me to create my quilts and my work is a sort of homage to the earth, a remembrance of times when life was simpler and slower, when we were children lying on our tummies, looking up through the grass at the insects or watching the birds in the trees. Appliqué allows me to recreate scenes like these in a way that plain piecing does not.

Whether using cotton fabric or felt, my appliqué designs try to capture the innocence and wonder of those times, and I find that my ideas are conveyed more readily through a folk-art style. Layering appliqué shapes, adding embroidery by machine or hand and then quilting, all play a part to create something beautiful. Drawing on a palette of soft, country colours there is sure to be something here to brighten up your home throughout the year. There are nineteen irresistible projects, from quick table mats and bags to more ambitious wall hangings and quilts.

At the back of the book the Techniques section describes all the hand and machine techniques needed for the projects, with emphasis on different types of appliqué, including needle turn and using freezer paper, templates and fusible web. Most of the projects use templates so before you start a project refer to Using Templates for important advice. All techniques and templates are listed in the Index, with their relevant page numbers.

Each project has instructions for the mix of techniques I used, but it's often possible to substitute other techniques, so a project using a hand appliqué method could use a machine method instead. Quilting can also be by hand or machine to suit your preference. With practise you will find what you like.

Measurements are in Imperial inches with metric conversions in brackets – use one or the other as they are not interchangeable. The most accurate results will be obtained using inches.

Whether you want to make a small project for a friend or a larger one to display in your own home the main thing is to take your time and enjoy yourself. Appliqué is very forgiving and you will be amazed and pleased at what you can achieve. You don't need to be too precise as to where the pieces are placed – that's also the beauty of a folk-art look. Keep a healthy balance between perfection and slapdash, and above all enjoy what you create.

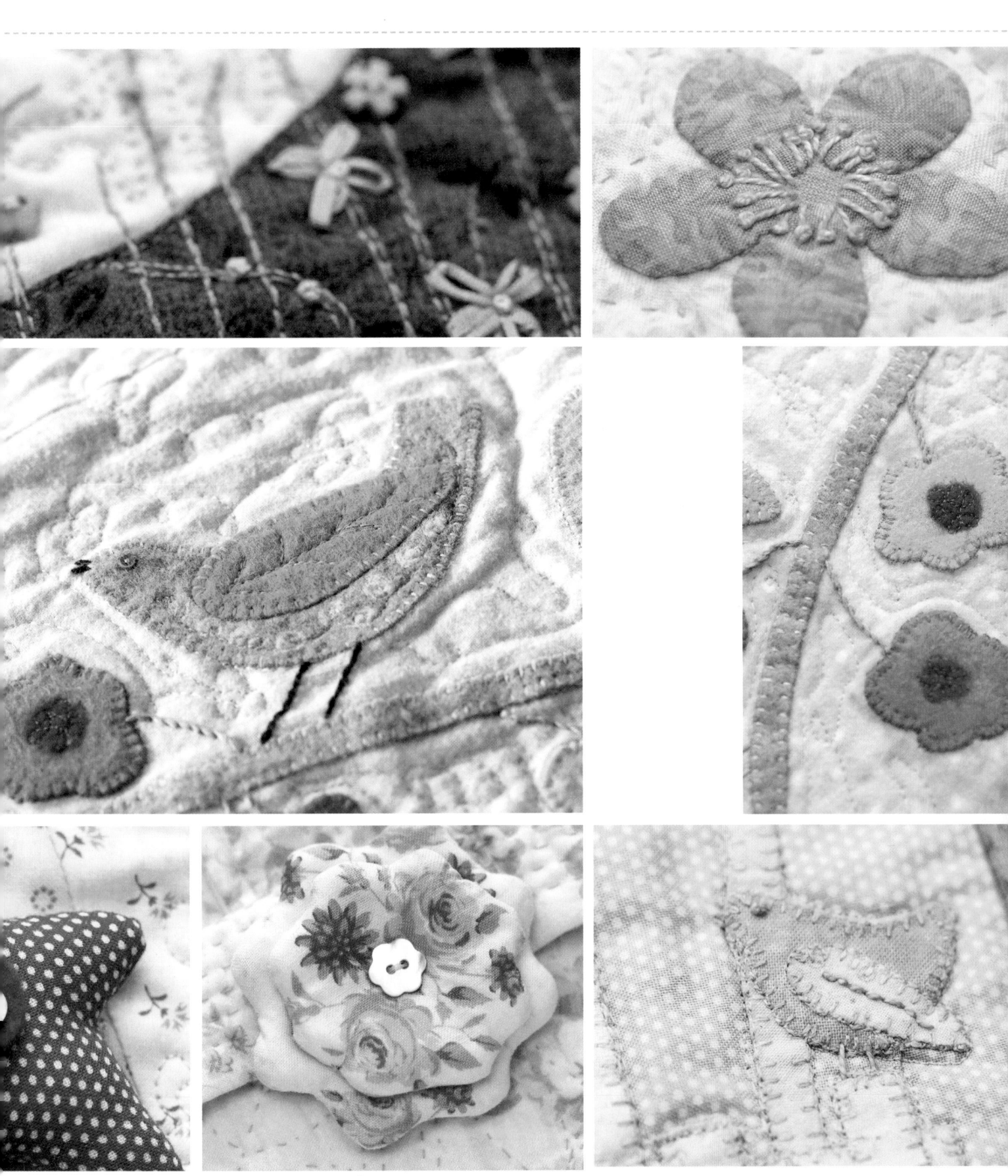

Fabric Selection

Choosing fabric is a vital, and exciting, part of making a quilt. It is also a very personal thing so be guided by what pleases you. The following advice will help.

Fabric Pattern

Most of my projects are picture-based appliqué. For these types of designs it is important for your eye to be able to see the shapes of the pieces and the overall picture clearly. Using fabrics with a large printed pattern is distracting and camouflages the shapes, so these fabrics are difficult to use successfully. I like to use tone-on-tone fabrics, those with small patterns that do not contrast too much with the background. Plain fabrics show the shapes very clearly and can be very dramatic, but they show every slightest mistake too. If I do use solids I usually add machine or hand embroidery.

Fabric Colour

Colour is probably the most important aspect of fabric and thread choice. Try to think of the fabrics and threads you choose as making up a paint box of colours. I tend to use a fairly small range of colours on a project, or more particularly a small number of colour families. Rainbow colours have their place but probably not for my quilts. Fabrics will tend to go together well if you can see one of the colours in one fabric echoed in the other.

When you are planning how the fabrics will fit together for the quilt, consider the balance of colours over the whole quilt, and similarly the balance of light and dark. See how the different colours 'play' against each other and consider whether a particular area in a quilt needs contrast or harmony. Sometimes you can see these aspects more clearly with your eyes half shut.

For appliqué choose fabrics with small patterns that don't have too many colours in them. Tone-on-tone fabrics are wonderful for this. The odd fabric can have a larger pattern that can be fussy cut into a flower or circle.

Fabric Types

Although people use all sorts of fabrics, I suggest you stick to those that have been designed for quilting because they will be a good weight, easy to sew through and easy to quilt. Use 100% cottons and as high a quality as you can afford. When appliquéing small shapes you will need to choose fabrics that don't fray too much and aren't too thick. If a fabric you like does fray and you don't want to use a different one, then allow extra around the shapes.

To Wash or Not?

None of the fabrics used in this book were pre-washed. I like the crispness of new fabric and the effect of washing a finished quilt, when the whole shrinks a little to give a puffed look. However, although it has never happened to me, fabrics can bleed and ruin a project. For this reason I'm careful with strong reds. If in doubt test fabrics first, pre-wash them or dry clean the finished project. This is another reason to buying a well-known make of fabric. Note that in some cases the measurement for a piece assumes the full width of a bolt or fat quarter. In these cases, of course, pre-washing might cause problems with shrinkage.

For felt projects some people recommend pre-washing to avoid shrinking later. It also changes the texture in a way you may like. If you do this, then allow an extra 20–30% for the quantity measurements, as felt shrinks in the wash by an unpredictable amount. Personally, I would not risk washing the finished project, but only dry clean it. I tend to be particularly cautious about felt colours and avoid deep reds and browns, as these are more likely to bleed.

Blending fabrics together so that they harmonize beautifully, especially the tones found in nature, helps create a coherent and most attractive look to a project.

Drying in the Breeze

This quilt wall hanging depicts a moment in time in a lovely rural setting – a country house, plump geese in the field and two delightful little quilts drying in the breeze on a washing line in the orchard. Divided into appliqué panels in beautifully blended colours, the quilt is straightforward to create and a joy to stitch.

The project has a little bit of everything and is a wonderful way of trying new techniques, including invisible machine appliqué, machine piecing, foundation piecing, free-motion quilting and hand embroidery. The design is versatile too – you could stitch the whole design or just focus on one of the panels for a smaller wall hanging. The quilt can also be made using hand appliqué techniques, as the alternative quilt shown in this chapter has been.

APPLIQUE FOCUS...

Geese are created with simplified shapes, using invisible machine appliqué after making the shapes with freezer paper. Overlapping wings creates extra texture.

Appliqué with bias-cut fabric strips makes sewing curved shapes easier and was used to create flower stems. The fencing uses straight grain strips.

The leaves are created with template plastic and invisible machine-stitched appliqué in easy shapes, with a little backstitch hand embroidery for the twig detail.

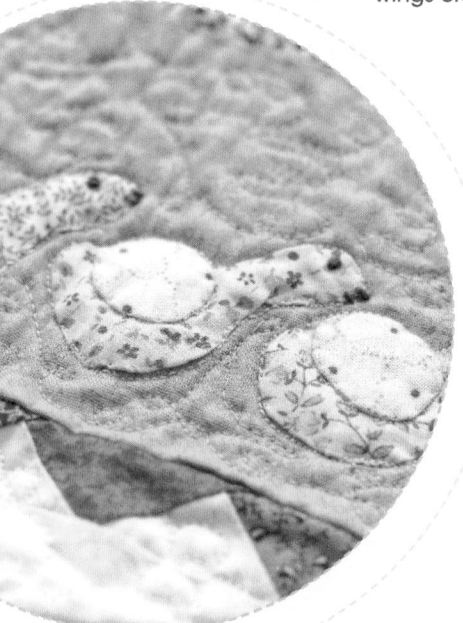

This gorgeous wall quilt would be a lovely centrepiece in any home. It is full of interesting details and with its sweet little quilts hanging on the washing line is sure to be much admired.

Drying in the Breeze Quilt

YOU WILL NEED

- Background fabric for main panels, end panels and triangle strips 42in x 23½in (106.7cm x 59.7cm)
- Fabric for border triangles 42in x 12in (106.7cm x 30.5cm)
- Inner border 30in x 5in (76.2cm x 12.7cm)
- Border blocks, nine different fabrics each 21in x 5½in (53.3cm x 14cm)
- Panel 1 hill fabric 20¾in x 4½in (52.7cm x 11.4cm)
- Flower stems 9in x 9in (22.9cm x 22.9cm)
- Large leaves on stems 21in x 9¾in (53.3cm x 24.8cm)
- Scraps of numerous different fabrics for small appliqués
- Scraps of different fabrics for the mini quilts
- Backing and binding 42in x 43in (106.7cm x 109.2cm)
- Wadding (batting) 42in x 33in (106.7cm x 83.8cm)
- Invisible thread for the appliqué
- Embroidery thread for twigs, windows, mini quilt and bird features in colours to suit your fabrics
- Four miniature clothes pegs for mini quilts
- Cord for washing line 23in (58.4cm) ·
- Basic kit

Finished size: 38in x 29in (96.5cm x 73.7cm)
Techniques used: freezer paper appliqué, invisible machine appliqué, appliquéd strips, foundation piecing, hand embroidery, free-motion quilting, binding Use ¼in (6mm) seams for the main quilt
Templates: Drying in the Breeze

Making panel 1

1 Cut out the background fabric 20¾in x 10in (52.7cm x 25.4cm). This includes a seam allowance. If you worry about fraying, or that the pieced outer border may not come out exactly the right size, you can make the rectangle a little bigger and trim later. The finished size for Panel 1 will be 20¼in x 9½in (51.4cm x 24.1cm).

Sewing the appliqués

2 Enlarge the templates to full size. Take care with the order you add the appliqué pieces so that any overlapping works properly. Make two strips of fencing 13½in (34.3cm) long (left of house) and 7½in (19cm) long (right of house). Make them in the same way as stems – see Appliquéd Strips. Cut each of the strips into four. Appliqué the cross pieces of the fence first, making sure their ends will just be covered by the house. Add the fence posts, making sure that the bottoms will just be covered by the hill.

3 Prepare the house walls and roof for appliqué using the Freezer Paper Underneath method. Join them to each other by hand first and then appliqué them to the background, making sure the base of the walls will just be covered by the hill. Using the Freezer Paper on Top method add the door, windows and chimney, making sure the base of the door will be covered by the hill. Add the hill

(freezer paper under) and turn the top raw edge over the paper as normal but leave the sides and bottom raw. The bottom of the hill should be in line with the bottom of the background fabric. Add the geese, bodies and then wings (freezer paper under).

4 Add the stems for the large flowers, followed by flower heads and leaves. To make each flower place two 5½in (14cm) squares right sides together. Draw the flower shape in the centre of one of the squares, on the back. Sew all the way round the drawn line and cut the flower out with ¼in (6mm) seam allowance. Snip into the curves and snip a hole in the centre of the flower. Turn inside out and press. Position the flowers so that they cover the end of the stem and machine in place. Add the leaves using template plastic and the Appliqué using Templates method. Using two strands of embroidery thread, embroider the windows using backstitch and the geese features with two small parallel stitches and a French knot eye.

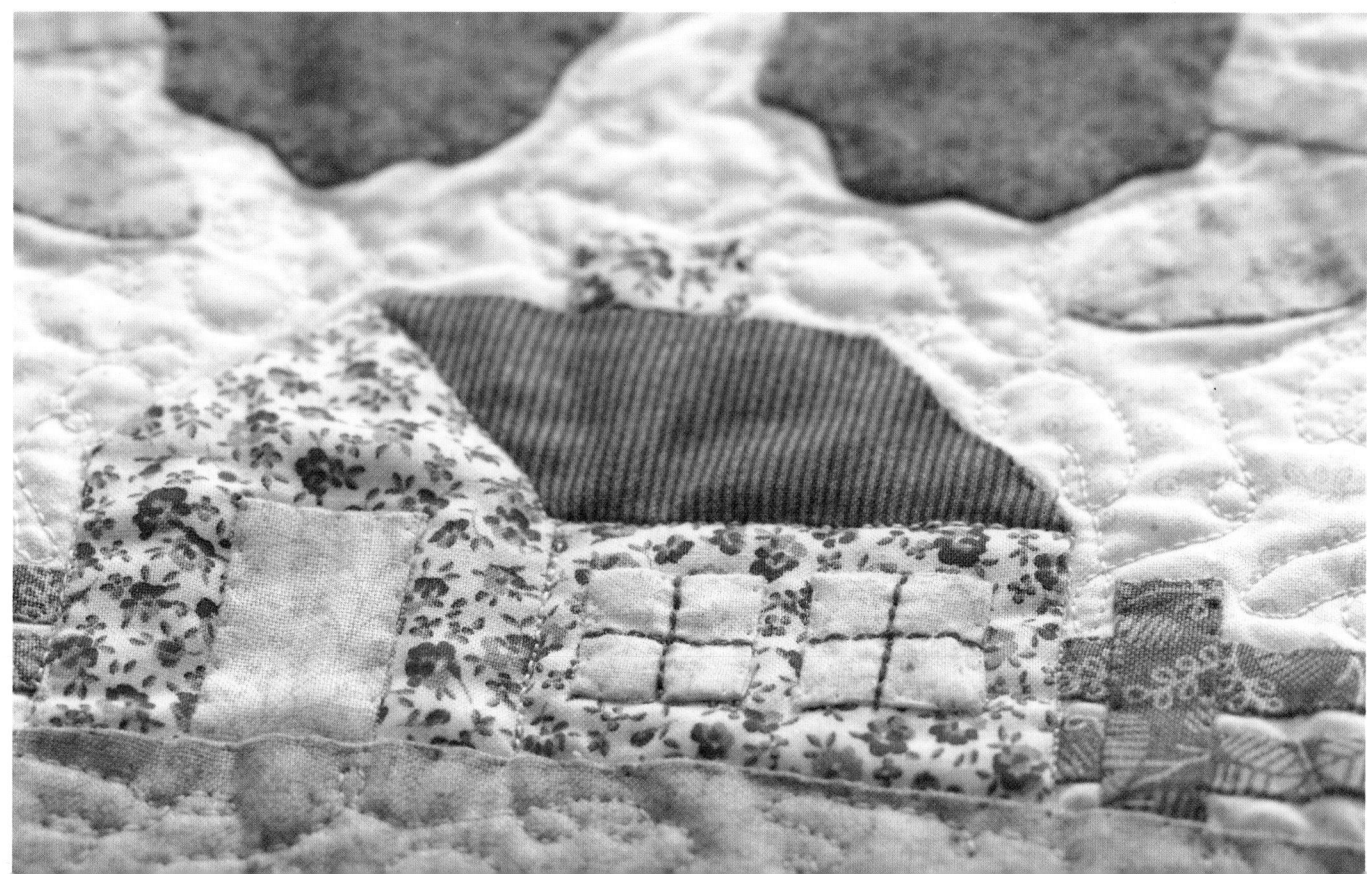

Making panel 2

5 Cut out the background fabric 20¾in x 10¼in (52.7cm x 26cm). This allows for a seam. Again, if you want more allowance make the rectangle bigger. The finished size for panel 2 will be 20¼in x 9¾in (51.4cm x 24.8cm).

Sewing the appliqués

6 For the tree branches and trunk use the Freezer Paper on Top method. Number all the branches on the template and on the freezer paper to help keep track of the pieces. Follow this order to add the pieces.

a Small branches first, making sure the large branches will overlap the end of the small branches.

b Sew on the large branches, making sure the trunk will overlap them and that the tree trunks end ¼in (6mm) below the bottom of the drawn rectangle.

c Using template plastic or freezer paper prepare the leaves in a variety of different greens and sew them in place.

d Add the bird.

Using two strands of thread, embroider the twigs of the trees in back stitch and the bird's beak using two small parallel stitches, and the eye as a French knot.

Making the top and bottom panels

7 Cut two pieces of background fabric each 20¾in x 4¼in (52.7cm x 10.8cm) (includes a ¼in/6mm seam). Leave more allowance if you wish and trim later. The finished size for these end panels is 20¼in x 3¾in (51.4cm x 9.5cm).

Sewing the appliqués

8 To help place the appliqué pieces for the flowers, fold each piece of fabric in half both ways and steam iron to crease. Prepare the appliqué pieces. Add the stems – each is 7½in (19cm) long. See Appliquéd Strips. Add the flower heads and leaves.

This variation of the quilt was worked entirely with hand appliqué using a more mellow colour scheme. It is very similar to the quilt described in the instructions but with an additional lower panel. The templates for this variation are available from my website: www.clarespatterns.co.uk

Making the triangle strips

9 The strips of triangles that go between the panels are made with foundation piecing. Make a plastic triangle using the foundation piecing template. Note: the template shows the *cutting*, not the sewing line. Use it to mark out triangles, making sure that the longest side of the triangle is either along the grain of the fabric or at right angles to it. You will need forty-eight triangles from the main background fabric and forty-eight from various red/pink scraps, using perhaps eight different fabrics. Place the triangles on a work top so they are arranged alternately, pink, background, pink, background, and so on.

10 There are three strips of triangles altogether. Trace the template for the strips three times on to paper. Using these paper templates, join the triangles into strips using foundation piecing – see Foundation Piecing Triangle Strips. There are thirty-two triangles in each strip.

Joining the panels and strips

11 Using a ¼in (6mm) seam, sew the strips to the main panels and end panels. When you join the triangle strips it is important that the seam does not cut off the points of the triangles. It may help to place a pin through the panel and strip exactly where each triangle point is.

Making the outer border

12 The wide outer border is made up of twenty-eight nine-patch blocks, which are joined together with triangles. If the match between the sizes of the outer and inner borders is not exact, there is some scope for adjustment by changing the size of the inner border. For this reason it is a good idea not to add the inner border until after the outer border is made. Choose nine different fabrics and cut twenty-eight 1½in (3.8cm) squares from each (252 in total). Collect the squares into groups of nine, with all nine fabrics in each group. Sew the groups of nine squares into nine-patch blocks, so you have twenty-eight blocks, each 3½in (8.9cm) square to its raw edges – see Fig 1.

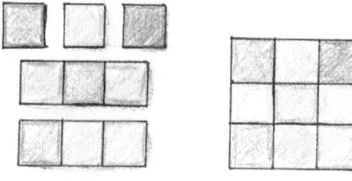

Fig 1 Nine-patch block

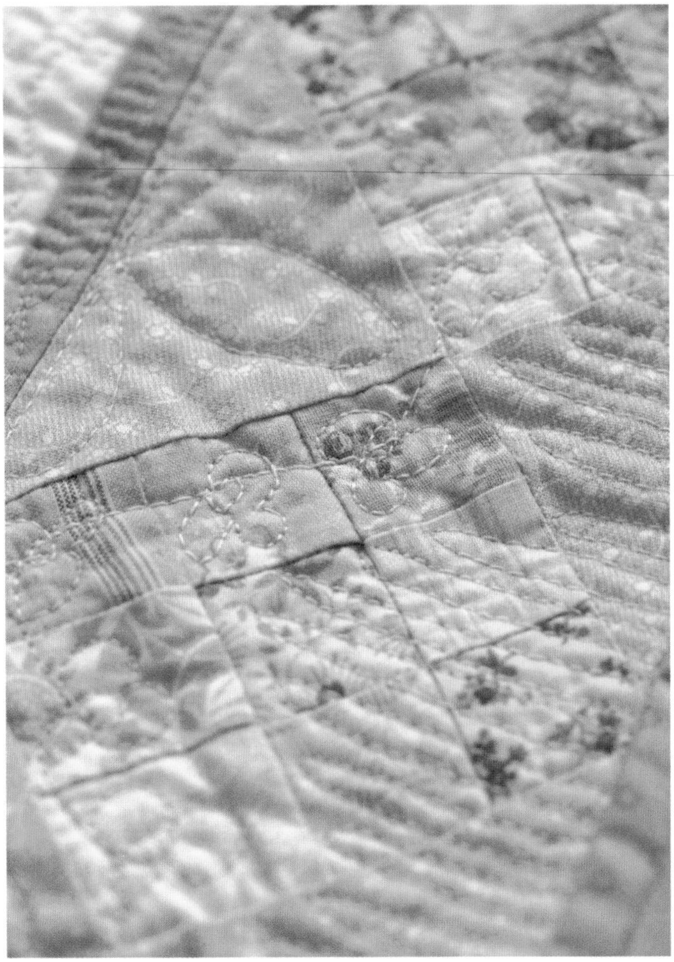

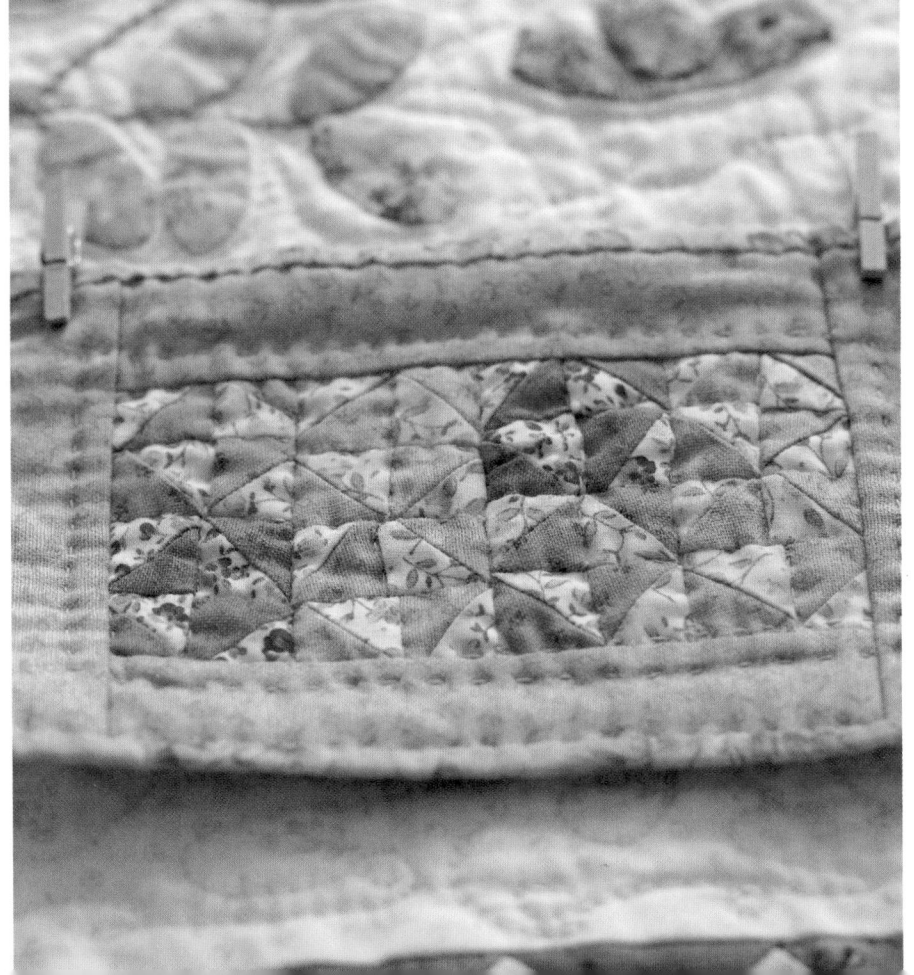

13 From the fabric chosen for the border triangles, cut twelve 5½in (14cm) squares. Cut each square across both diagonals to create forty-eight triangles in total. Sew these triangles to the nine-patch blocks to make the border (see Fig 2). Make separate border sections for the two sides, the two ends and the corners, as shown, and set aside.

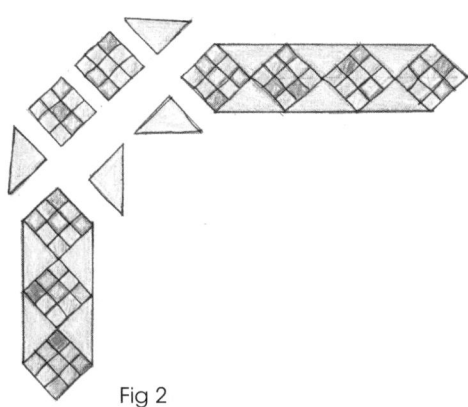

Fig 2

Adding the borders

14 Check that the centre of the quilt and the outer border fit, with room for a ½in (1.3cm) finished inner border between them. If they don't fit perfectly, adjust the width of the inner border appropriately. Add this inner border – see Adding a Border. Now sew on the outer border side pieces, followed by the top and bottom pieces and finally the four corner sections (Fig 3).

Fig 3

Quilting and binding

15 Create the quilt sandwich – see Making a Quilt Sandwich. I used a spray glue. Quilt as you wish – see Quilting. I used free-motion machine quilting in a 'swirly' pattern on the panels and main border and also some leaves, flowers and lines.

16 Finish off the quilt by binding all round the outside – see Binding.

Making the left-hand mini quilt

17 Both little quilts are made by piecing with a ⅛in (3mm) seam allowance. Cut 1in (2.5cm) squares: sixteen dark (four different fabrics), sixteen light (four different fabrics). Make half-square triangle units as follows. Place a dark and a light square right sides together and draw a line across a diagonal. Draw a line on either side of the diagonal ⅛in (3mm) away (see Fig 4). Sew along the two lines and cut through the middle line to make two squares, each with two contrasting triangles. Press the seam to one side. Repeat with the other squares for eight half-square triangles in total. Sew four together, light against dark. Repeat with the other colours. Sew them all together.

Fig 4 Half-square triangles

18 For the border cut two pieces 4½in x 1in (11.4cm x 2.5cm) and two 3¾in x 1in (9.5cm x 2.5cm). Sew on the longer pieces first and then the shorter ones. Trim if necessary.

19 Cut wadding (batting) the same size as the little quilt. Cut a piece of fabric ½in (1.3cm) bigger all the way round than the quilt. Place the wadding and then the quilt on top of the backing so there is ½in (1.3cm) extra all the way round. Fold the raw edge over to the quilt front, and fold over again. Sew it down, creating a binding all round.

Making the right-hand mini quilt

20 Cut sixteen 1in (2.5cm) squares in different colours. Join them together in rows of four. It helps to draw a line ⅛in (3mm) away from the raw edges for the correct seam allowance. For the border cut two pieces 2¼in x 1in (5.7cm x 2.5cm) and two 3½in x 1in (8.9cm x 2.5cm). Join the shorter pieces on first, then the longer ones.

21 Embroider backstitch, lazy daisy stitch and French knots on the quilt – see pictures. Add wadding and backing and finish the edges as before.

22 Fold your piece of cord in half and sew the mini quilts to it so they are on either side of the halfway point. Place against the large quilt to gauge how long the washing line should be then knot each end of the line. Sew to the tree trunks to finish.

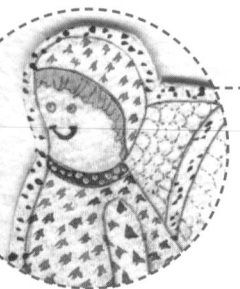

Christmas Angel

This sweet angel has a Scandinavian look, with her cream colouring and dashes of red, and is a perfect project to make for yourself or a friend. Her skirt is made up of curved panels, with folded triangles at her waist. She wears a simple hat and cute felt shoes with buttons and bows. Machine quilting decorates her wings, dress and hat. Techniques used include simple curved piecing using freezer paper, binding on the bias, machine quilting and making stuffed stars.

There are also two boxes in this chapter on a red and white theme – perfect for housing treats at Christmas time. When in use they are tied into shape with tags but can be stored flat. They are reversible and are made using board pocketed in fabric. One box has English paper-pieced stars and appliquéd circles. The other uses buttons, with the stars and large circles sewn down with embroidery stitches.

APPLIQUE FOCUS...

Simple hand embroidery creates the doll's face, peeping out from under felt hair and a machine quilted hat.

The angel doll holds a cluster of appliquéd stars and hearts made from bright, festive fabrics.

A strip of folded triangles adds a splash of colour and interest to the waistband of the angel's dress.

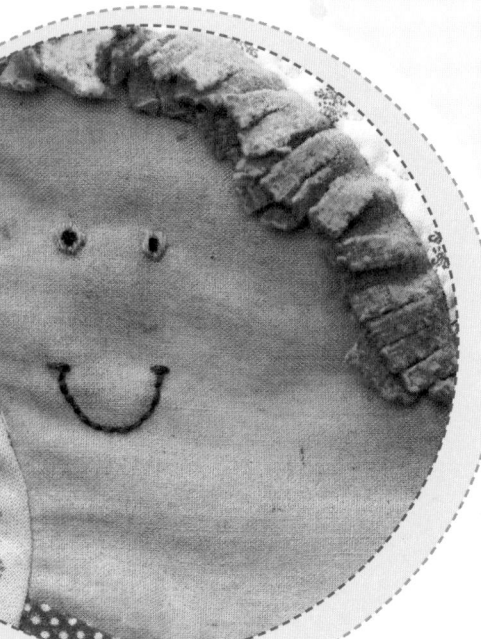

This sweet doll would make a perfect Christmas gift for a little girl or to bring out and display every year as part of the Christmas decorations.

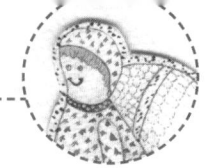

Angel Doll

1 Enlarge the templates to full size. Make a reverse tracing of all the pieces on the templates.

YOU WILL NEED

- Fabric for wings 12in x 7in (30.5cm x 17.8cm)
- Fabric for face, hands, legs 19½in x 12in (49.5cm x 30.5cm)
- Fabric for dress panels 1, 5 and 9 and hat, bodice and arms 21in x 16in (53.3cm x 40.6cm)
- Fabric for dress panels 4, 8 and 12: 15in x 12in (38.1cm x 30.5cm)
- Fabric for dress panels 3, 7 and 11: 15in x 11½in (38.1cm x 29.2cm)
- Fabric for dress panels 2, 6 and 10: 15in x 11in (38.1cm x 27.9cm)
- Felt/brushed cotton for hair 5in x 3½in (12.7cm x 8.9cm)
- Fabric for collar, triangles round waist, star, band 18in x 6in (45.7cm x 15.2cm)
- Fabric for second star 8in x 4in (20.3cm x 10.2cm)
- Felt for shoes and hearts on stars 8in x 8in (20.3cm x 20.3cm)
- Backing fabric 27in x 17in (68.6cm x 43.2cm)
- Binding fabric 12in x 12in (30.5cm x 30.5cm)
- Wadding (batting) 27in x 17in (68.6cm x 43.2cm)
- Toy stuffing
- Ribbon ¼in (6mm) wide x 22in (56cm) long
- Three small buttons and one medium button
- Embroidery thread in colours to suit your fabrics
- Basic kit

Finished size: 24in x 16in (61cm x 41cm)
Techniques used: freezer paper templates, machine sewing, quilting, binding
Use ¼in (6mm) seams throughout
Templates: Angel Doll

Cutting out the skirt
2 The skirt is made up of twelve different panels, machine sewn together. There are four different fabrics which are repeated three times. Draw all the panel shapes on to freezer paper. Number the pieces one to twelve on your traced drawing and your freezer paper pieces. Note that number 1 is nearest the wing. This numbering is important as the panels are all different.

3 Cut out the freezer paper pieces and iron them on to the appropriate fabric. Cut around each shape leaving ¼in (6mm) all around for seams. Don't remove the freezer paper yet.

4 Cut out the four 2in (5.1cm) squares that will make the triangles at the waist. Cut out a band measuring 17in x 1in (43.2cm x 2.5cm).

Sewing the skirt
5 All the panels are sewn together with the thin ends at the top and the wider ends at the bottom. Using the edges of the paper on each piece as a guide, pin the numbered pieces together with the paper facing outwards. Machine sew along the edge of the paper ¼in (6mm) in from the raw edges. Continue in this way from left to right, joining all the panels together. Press the skirt and remove the freezer paper.

6 Take the four 2in (5.1cm) square pieces and fold each point to point, forming a triangle. Fold each triangle again to make a smaller triangle. Pin or.tack (baste) these triangles along the top of the skirt so the raw edge lines up with the top of the skirt. Hand sew the band to the bottom of the skirt 1in (2.5cm) up from the raw edge.

Making the bodice and triangles

7 Trace the bodice on to freezer paper and cut out along the drawn line. Iron on to the back of the bodice fabric and cut out allowing ¼in (6mm) for a seam allowance. Peel the freezer paper off. Sew it to the skirt, making sure that the triangles you just tacked (basted) to the skirt are sandwiched between the bodice and the skirt.

Making the head

8 Trace the head and hat on to freezer paper, as before and cut out. Cut out a strip for the collar 3½in x 1in (8.9cm x 2.5cm), cut on the bias. Line up the head so that it overlaps with the neck of the bodice and sew them together. Cover the raw edges with the collar, tucking in the edges as you go.

9 Cut out a 5in x 3½in (12.7cm x 8.9cm) piece for the hair and fold it in half lengthways and sew all along ¼in (6mm) in from the fold. With scissors cut a series of snips in from the raw edge almost up to the sewing line. Make a series of ¼in (6mm) snips into the concave side of the hat. Pin it in position on top of the head with the snipped edge tucked under. Now tuck the hair between the hat and the face and sew all three together by hand, making sure you sew right through to the head.

Making the wing

10 Trace the wing on to freezer paper. Cut out and iron on to the fabric as described before. Cut out the wing with a ¼in (6mm) seam allowance. Peel off the freezer paper. Sew the wing on to the bodice and skirt (the angel's back is the side where panel 1 was sewn).

Making the legs and shoes

11 Cut out four pieces of fabric for the legs each 5½in x 4½in (14cm x 11.4cm). Trace four leg shapes on to freezer paper (two reversed). Cut them out and iron on to the back of the 5½in x 4½in pieces. Cut them out with ¼in (6mm) seam allowance. Pair them, right sides together, so you have a left pair and a right pair. Leave one freezer paper shape on each pair. Trace four shoe shapes on to freezer paper. Cut out and pin the shapes on to the felt. Cut out each shape with a ¼in (6mm) seam allowance.

12 To make each leg sandwich the legs and shoes together in the following order:

a Leg without freezer paper facing up.

b Two felt shoes.

c Leg with freezer paper facing up.

Pin the sandwich together. Machine round sewing right up to the paper, leaving the top open. Snip into the seam allowance round the curves. Turn inside out and stuff with toy stuffing. Add some ribbon, folding in the raw edges and sew in place with a button. Put aside for the moment.

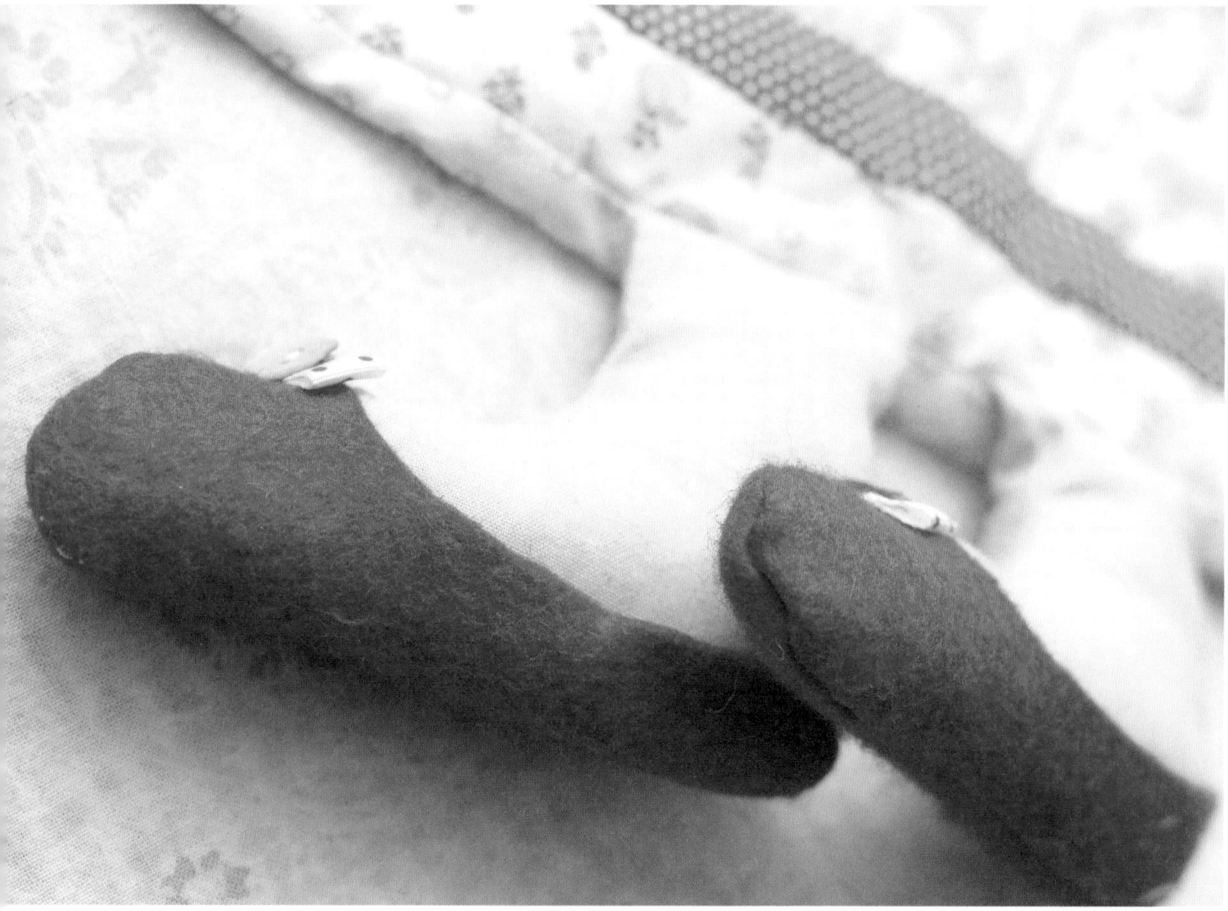

Making the arm

13 Trace and cut out of freezer paper two arm shapes (one reversed) and two hand shapes (one reversed). Sew each arm to a hand, making sure the thumbs face upwards. Place the two hands and arms together, right side inwards, and sew all around leaving the top open. Turn right side out and fill the arm with toy filling, leaving about ½in (1.3cm) at the top. Turn the raw edge at the top inwards and sew the opening together. (Note that the arm is not added to the angel until after the quilting.)

Making the stars

14 From two different fabrics cut a rectangle 8in x 4in (20.3cm x 10.2cm). Fold each rectangle in half right sides together so that they measure 4in (10.2cm) square.

15 Trace two star shapes on to freezer paper and cut them out. Iron each star in the middle of the 4in (10.2cm) square. Cut two pieces of ribbon 7in (17.8cm) and 10in (25.4cm) long. Fold in half and place between the two layers, with the ribbon ends poking out slightly above the raw edge of the top of the star.

16 Pin and machine sew right up to the freezer paper, leaving a gap in order to turn inside out. Stuff with toy stuffing and sew up the gap.

17 For each star cut out a felt heart and sew to the middle of the star with the button. Secure the ribbons to the angel's hand. Embroider the mouth with two strands of red embroidery thread and backstitch. Work the eyes in tiny satin stitches in blue in a circular shape, with a black French knot in the centre, or use little buttons for eyes.

Quilting and binding

18 Refer to Making a Quilt Sandwich and Quilting in the technique section. Quilt the panels, bodice, hat and wings. The top half of the wing shape is the wing behind, so quilt this part first. With a pencil draw a curved line where the bias strip is to be placed. When quilting the wings I quilted a row, stopped, pulled thread through to the front for sewing in later, and then moved the needle to start the next row. When the quilting is finished, sew on the arm.

19 Cut 1¼in (3.2cm) wide strips on the bias to a length of about 90in (230cm). Sew a bias strip the same colour as the binding where the two wings meet to give the impression of two wings. Line up the raw edges of the leg with the raw edges of the skirt so that the legs look upside down (see Fig 1). Pin the legs in place. When sewing on the binding sew in the legs at the same time. Sew all the way around to finish the doll.

Fig 1

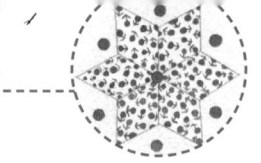

Treats Box

Preparing the board and wadding

1 Using a craft knife cut the grey board into one 10in (25.4cm) square and four pieces 10in x 4in (25.4cm x 10.2cm). Cut the wadding (batting) into one piece 10in x 20in (25.4cm x 50.8cm) and four pieces 10in x 8in (25.4cm x 20.3cm). Take each piece of card and wrap the corresponding piece of wadding around it tightly. Over sew the wadding round all the board pieces.

Preparing star and circle appliqués

2 Make six diamond templates for the large star and twelve diamond templates for the small stars using thick paper. English paper piece one large star and two small stars following the instructions in English Paper Piecing.

3 Make two large circles, two medium and nineteen small circles using washers and template plastic – see Appliqué Using Templates.

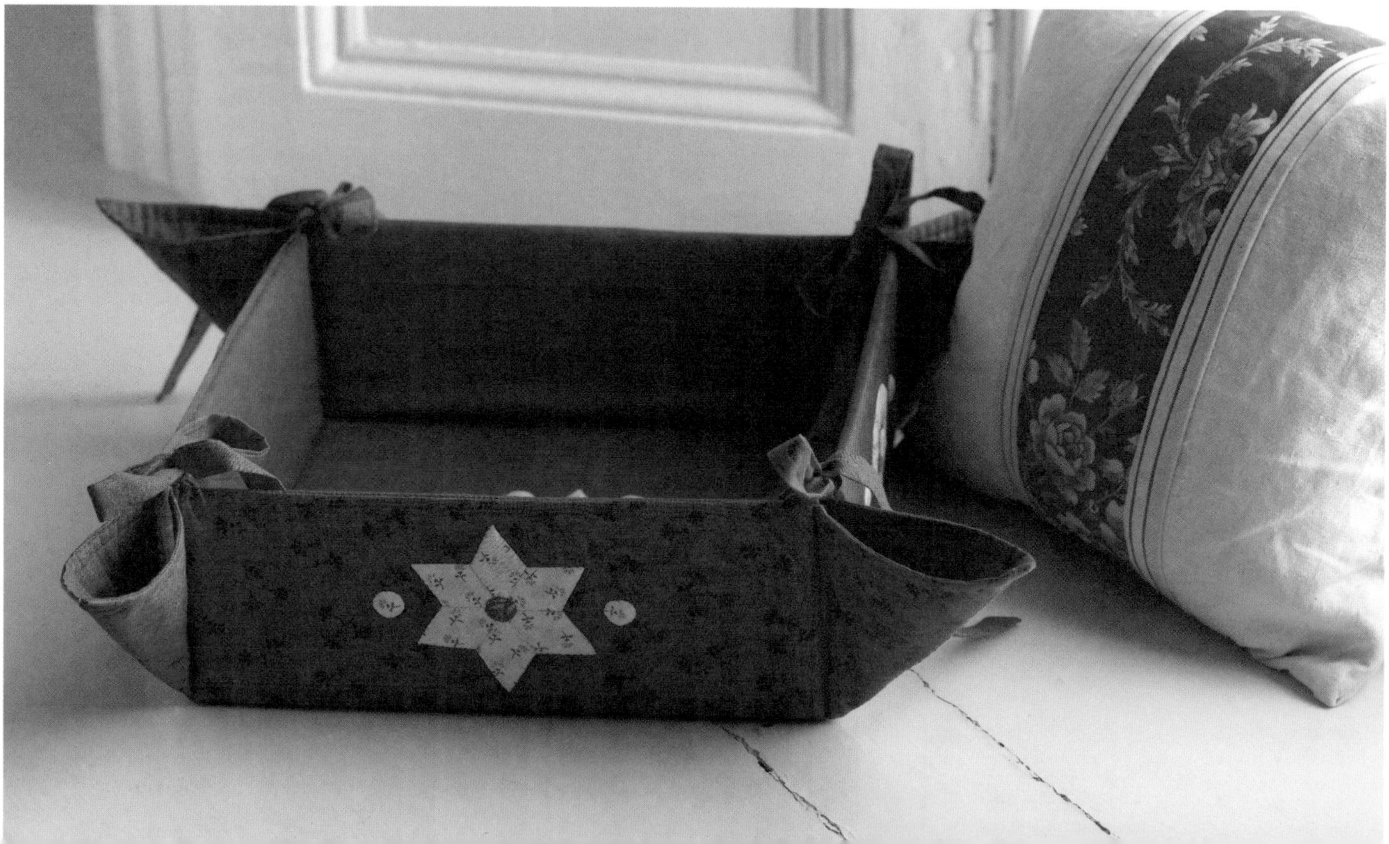

Preparing background and lining

4 Cut a 19½in (49.5cm) square of background fabric and the same from lining. For both fabric pieces, make a hem along one side by placing the pieces face down and lining up the edge of the ruler ¼in (6mm) in from one of the raw edges. Crease along the edge with a tool such as a hera. Fold the fabric over, press and tack (baste) down.

Appliquéing the stars and circles

5 The lining has an appliqué star in the middle and each side of the box has a star or a circle in the centre on the outside. In order to find these centres, fold the lining and the background pieces neatly in half and half again at right angles. Press to get the creases at a cross in the middle and crease lines right up to the raw edge.

6 For the lining, line up the centre of the star with the creased cross on the fabric. Pin and sew in place. Sew six small circles evenly around the star.

7 For the background, sew the two stars opposite each other, lining up the star points with the crease line ¾in (1.9cm) below the raw edge. Sew three small circles in place – one in a contrasting colour in the star centre and the other two, the same colour as the star, on either side.

8 Sew the large circles opposite each other on the other crease line 1¼in (3.2cm) in from the raw edge. Sew the medium circles on top of the large circles in a contrasting fabric, followed by the small circle. Sew a small circle on either side of the large circle. Press the background and lining fabric.

9 Cut four pieces of wadding (batting) each 4¾in (12.1cm) square. Line them up with the corners of the back of the lining fabric. Tack (baste) in place.

Making the ties

10 From the background fabric cut eight strips each 14in x 1½in (35.6cm x 3.8cm). Fold each piece in half right sides together lengthwise. Machine across one end and all the way down one side ⅛in (3mm) from the edge. Turn inside out and press.

11 Each side has two ties that are sandwiched between the background and the lining. They are sewn in place (the raw edge end) when the background and the lining are sewn together into a 'bag'. Lay the background face up. On three of the sides (not the side with the hem) place a tie 4¾in (12.1cm) in from the corner edge (see Fig 1). There are six ties in all. Pin and tack (baste).

Joining background and lining

12 Place the background and the lining pieces right sides together, with the tacked-on ties sandwiched between them and the corner wadding on top (Fig 2). Line up both hemmed edges well and pin both pieces together. Machine round three of the sides, leaving the hemmed edge unsewn. This fixes the ties as well as joining the background to the lining.

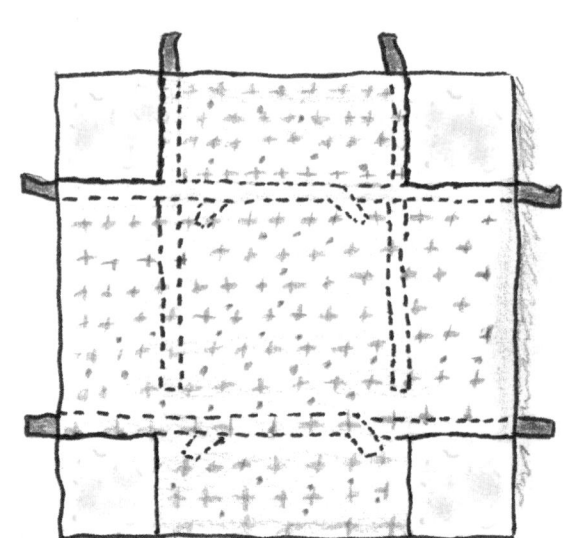

Fig 2

Fig 1

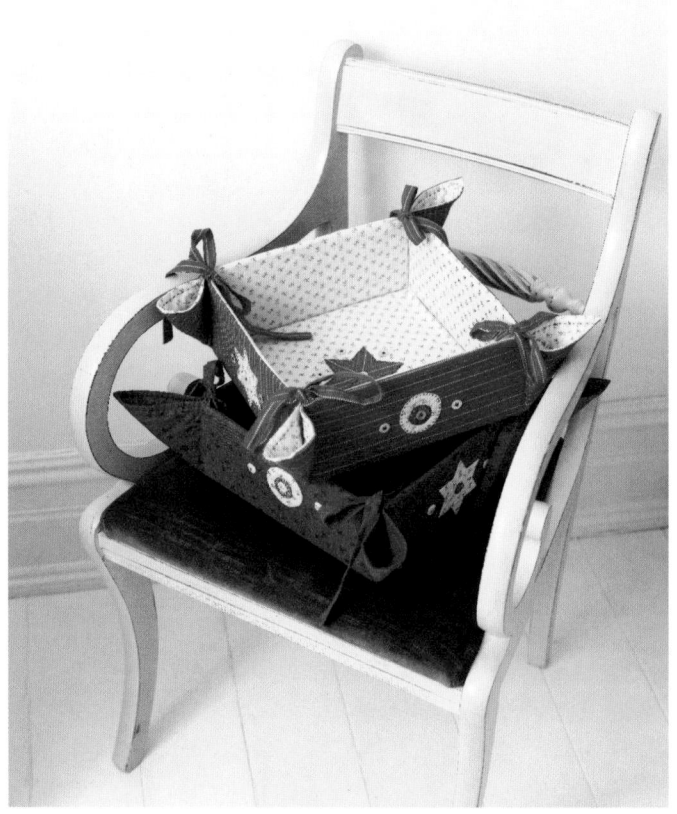

13 Turn inside out. Press flat and ensure the corners are well turned out. Undo the tacking on the ties, so now you have a bag with six ties sticking outwards.

Making pockets for cardboard

14 Place the 'bag' you have made on a table with the opening facing you. Line the ruler up 4³⁄₈in (11.1cm) from the left-hand edge, against the ties, and make a crease line all the way along the ruler (Fig 3) – a hera is useful for this. Turn the fabric round so the opening is furthest away from you and make another crease. Machine along

these creased lines. Turn the fabric round again so that the opening is on the right. Again, line the ruler up 4³⁄₈in (11.1cm) from the left-hand edge against the ties and make a crease line all the way along the ruler, at right angles to the other lines.

15 Slip one of the 10in x 4in (25.4cm x 10.2cm) cardboard pieces into the centre pocket so it fits snugly at the end. Machine sew along the crease line. Line the ruler up against the edge where the opening is and make a crease line 4³⁄₈in (11.1cm) in from the edge. Put the side pieces of cardboard and the centre piece in place, tucking them well in. Machine sew along the crease line. Place the final piece of cardboard in the pocket, tuck in the two remaining ties and pin the two pieces of fabric. Machine sew the two together. Quilt the corners with embroidery thread to finish.

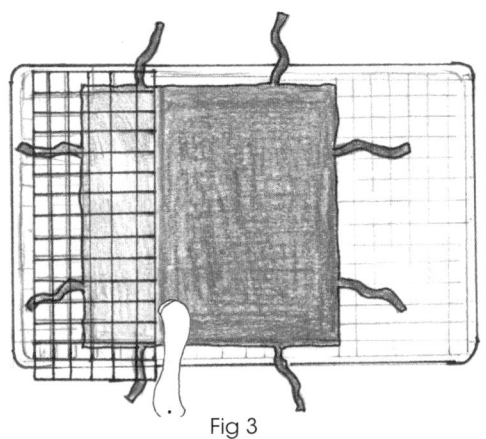

Fig 3

This alternative box use small buttons instead of appliquéd circles and the stars and large circles are sewn on with embroidery thread.

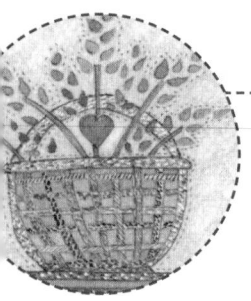

Woven Baskets

Baskets are not only functional and attractive additions to a home but can provide the inspiration for some lovely projects, and in this chapter a basket motif is used on a charming wall hanging and a cosy lap quilt. There are also some sweet little heart decorations to hang in your home.

The projects use the idea of an appliqué basket, where strips of fabric representing the weave of the basket are woven together as they are appliquéd to the background. You will have great fun mixing pretty fabrics together to make baskets of different colours. Hand appliqué is made easy with freezer paper and template plastic, while bias strips are used for flower stems. Stuffed appliqué is added for texture, plus some simple embroidery and shadow quilting.

APPLIQUE FOCUS...

The baskets in this chapter are created with strips of fabric appliquéd in a woven pattern, chosen to create a rustic appearance.

Templates were used for the flower appliqués on the wall hanging. The French knots in the centres add an extra decorative touch.

Easy stuffed appliqué produces an attractive three-dimensional quality and was used for a little heart to create more visual impact.

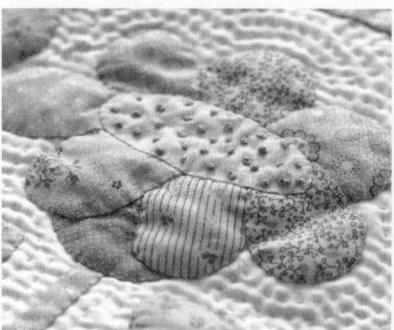
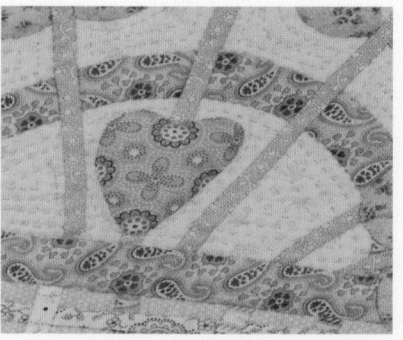

Woven appliqué strips create some beautiful baskets in this chapter. Use the technique on this delightful wall hanging or for the lovely Baskets Lap Quilt.

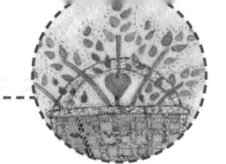

Basket on a Shelf Wall Hanging

YOU WILL NEED

- Background fabric 42in x 19½in (106.7cm x 49.5cm)
- Fabric for basket body 11½in x 6½in (29.2cm x 16.5cm)
- Basket top, handle, sides and base 12in x 8½in (30.5cm x 21.6cm)
- Warp and weft of basket fifteen strips of different fabrics each 11½in x ¾in (29.2cm x 1.9cm)
- Stems (cut on bias) from 9in x 9in (22.9cm x 22.9cm)
- Fabric for leaves 19½in x 7in (49.5cm x 17.8cm)
- Scraps of seven different fabrics for flowers
- Scrap of fabric for heart in basket
- Shelf fabric 16in x 8in (40.6cm x 20.3cm)
- Decorations hung from shelf:
  pink fabric for birds, medium heart, star and bird's wing 19½in x 5in (49.5cm x 12.7cm);
  red fabric for bird, large heart, small heart, birds' wings 10in x 7in (25.4cm x 17.8cm);
  blue circles 6in x 6in (15.2cm x 15.2cm)
- Border fabric 42in x 4in (106.7cm x 10.2cm)
- Toy stuffing
- Backing fabric 42in x 19½in (106.7cm x 49.5cm)
- Wadding (batting) 40in x 20in (101.6cm x 50.8cm)
- Binding fabric 8in x 42in (20.3cm x 106.7cm)
- Thread for embroidery and hand quilting thread (ecru)
- Basic kit

Finished size: 38in x 17½in (96.5cm x 44.5cm)

Techniques used: appliquéd strips, appliqué using freezer paper, appliqué using templates, stuffed appliqué, hand embroidery, shadow quilting, binding The project is made as two separate panels of a basket and a shelf with hanging decorations. Use ¼in (6mm) seams throughout

Templates: Basket on a Shelf Wall Hanging

Making the basket

1 Enlarge the templates to full size. Cut a piece of background fabric 17in (43.2cm) square. Cut out the basket body. Cut out the basket top strip, the handle and three strips for the sides and base. Cut out the strips to form the warp and weft of the basket 11½in (29.2cm) long – see Appliquéd Strips.

Weaving the warps and wefts

2 Put the three strips for the bottom and sides of the basket aside. Choose eight of the other strips and arrange them evenly across the basket body cut out earlier (these are the warps). I found it easiest to pin the basket body to a padded mat. Pin the warps as in Fig 1, with the pins out of the way above and below the basket body.

3 Take another seven strips to form the wefts, and weave them between the warps (Fig 2). Sew small tacks along the edge of the basket, sewing roughly but securely into place. These are important as they hold the whole thing together at this stage. If you want to do more tacking (basting) do so. Remove the pins.

4 Starting at the top, sew the wefts to the basket body using an over stitch. When you come to a warp, do a double stitch, slip the thread under the warp, do another double stitch on the other side and then continue (Fig 3). Carry on in this way until all the wefts are sewn down. Sew down the warps in the same way. Trim the excess from the ends of the strips so they line up with the edge of the basket body. Remove the tacking (basting).

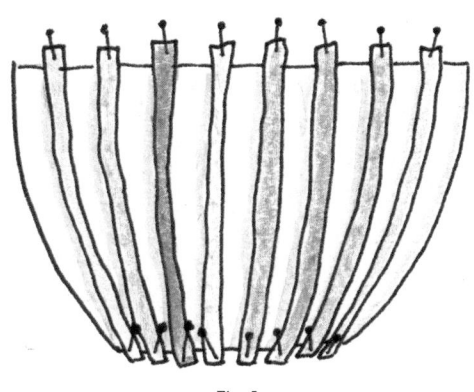

Fig 1

Leave space at the sides, the base and the top of the basket as these will be added later

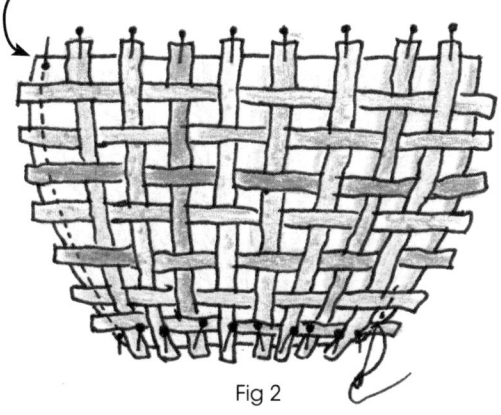

Fig 2

Fig 3

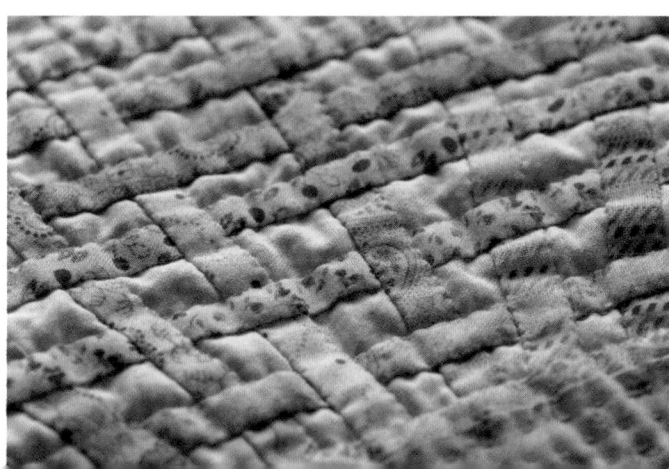

Adding the sides, top and bottom

5 Take the strips saved for the sides of the basket and sew them on so they just cover the raw edges of the body. Trim the excess. Add the strip for the bottom of the basket, with only one side of the strip turned under. The turned-under edge covers the raw edge of the body. The other edge stays raw and lines up with the edge of the background fabric.

6 Add the basket top strip, leaving the top of the strip unsewn so that you can slip in the ends of the stems. Overlap the top of the basket body by ¼in (6mm).

Sewing the basket to the background

7 Cut a 17in (43.2cm) square of background fabric. Pin and sew the basket centrally to this square, lining up the bottom of the basket with the raw edge of the square.

8 Pin and sew the handle in place, using the same folding technique to make sure it is in the middle, and slipping the ends under the basket top.

Appliquéing stems, leaves and flowers

9 Make the bias strips for the foliage and flower stems (as you made the warps and wefts, but cutting diagonally on the bias). Sew them on to the background using the picture as a guide, tucking them behind the basket. Sew the top of the basket to the background now. Note, you can trace the whole picture on to a fine interfacing such as Vilene or Pattern Ease. Put the Vilene drawing over the background fabric to see where to place everything.

10 Make the appliqué leaves (I used template plastic) and sew them in place. See Appliqué using Templates.

11 Make all the pieces for the flowers (I used freezer paper – see Appliqué using Freezer Paper). Remember to draw on the back of the template in order to reverse the flower so that when you sew on the pieces they are the right way round. Number all the petals on the template and on the freezer paper. Appliqué the flower bases first, then the petals, then the flower centre. It helps if you sew one flower at a time.

Adding the stuffed heart

12 Prepare the heart using template plastic. Remove the plastic and press well. Sew in place, leave a gap to insert some toy stuffing. Once stuffed, continue sewing.

Appliquéing the shelf

13 Cut out a piece of background fabric 17in x 23in (43.2cm x 58.4cm). Machine sew to the basket square, covering the raw edge of the bottom of the basket.

14 Prepare the shelf, drawing it on to freezer paper. Cut the freezer paper shelf out along the drawn line, and the heart too. Iron the freezer paper shape on to the back of your fabric. Cut out in the usual way with ¼in (6mm) seam allowance all round, fold over and press into place. Snipping into the seam allowance for the heart and on any curves before pressing will help the edges fold over neatly.

15 Appliqué half the shelf to the background, just covering the seam of the two background pieces at the top. Check that the shelf is in the centre of the background. Remove all the tacking and freezer paper and then sew the rest of the shelf and the heart.

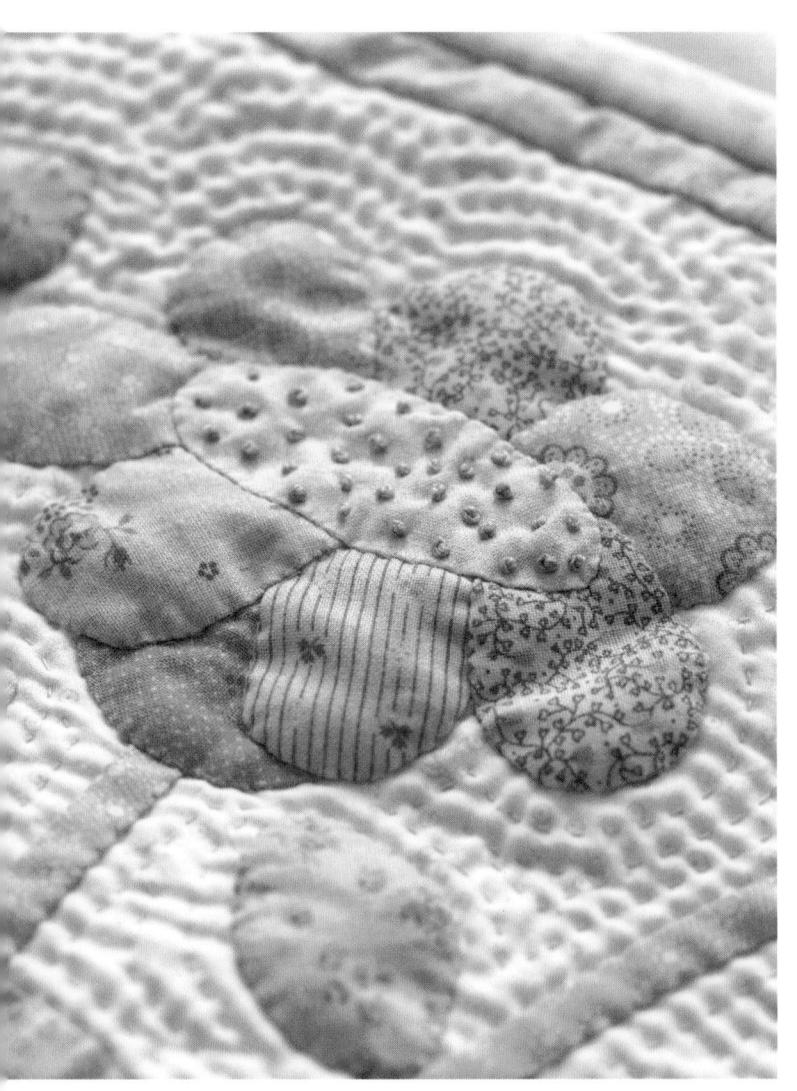

Appliquéing the hanging decorations

16 Prepare all the pieces for sewing on to the background. I used freezer paper for the birds, template plastic for the bird's wings and the hearts and a metal washer for the circles. Line them up by making two faint pencil lines corresponding to the strings holding the ornaments. Using two strands of embroidery thread, embroider two lines using stem stitch to represent the strings joining the decorations to each other and to the shelf (see Hand Embroidery).

Adding the border

17 Trim the quilt to 38in x 16½in (96.5cm x 42cm). Cut two pieces of fabric 38in x 1in (96.5cm x 2.5cm) and two pieces 17½in x 1in (44.5cm x 2.5cm) – or to sizes to fit your quilt, and sew to the quilt top. See Adding a Border for instructions.

Quilting and binding

18 Press the quilt and then follow the instructions in Making a Quilt Sandwich to fix the layers together ready for quilting.

19 Shadow quilt over the background, shelf, birds and heart. Quilt round the basket and the weaving, tucking the stitches right up to the appliqué and all round the flower, base, petals, flower centre, stems and leaves.

20 Finish your wall hanging with a binding as described in Binding. You will need to join three strips each 42in x 2½in (106.7cm x 6.4cm) long.

Baskets Lap Quilt

Finished size: 53in x 53in (134.6cm x 134.6cm)

Techniques used: appliquéd strips, appliqué using freezer paper, appliqué using templates, stuffed appliqué, hand embroidery, shadow quilting, binding Make the baskets in the same way as the Basket on a Shelf Wall Hanging, using the same template. Once familiar with the technique you could add more warps and wefts, as I did. Use ¼in (6mm) seams throughout

Templates: Baskets Lap Quilt

Sewing the centre four baskets

1 Make the centre baskets first as described in steps 1–6 of the Basket on a Shelf Wall Hanging. The baskets for the border are made slightly differently.

2 Cut four 17in (43.2cm) squares of background fabric. Pin and sew a basket to the centre of a background square (see Fig 1). To find the centre, fold both the square and the basket in half both ways and line up the creases. Leave the top of the basket unsewn for now. Pin and sew each handle in place, making sure it is in the middle. Sew the top of the basket to the background.

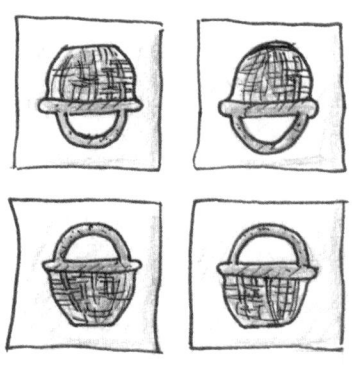

Fig 1

Sewing the stuffed areas

3 All the baskets have stuffed work between the handle and the basket. For the first four baskets this is done directly on the background fabric after the basket has been sewn on. For the outer four baskets it is done on a separate piece of background fabric which is then sewn on to the basket before the basket is sewn in place. Using the templates, draw the flower and the two leaves on to the background fabric (Fig 2). The positions of the petals and leaves are shown on the quilting template. Use a marker that can be removed. (Test markers on scrap fabric to make sure that the mark can be removed.)

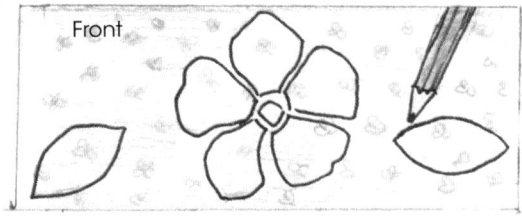

Fig 2

4 Place a piece of muslin on the back of your background fabric, behind the drawing, covering the drawing with space to spare. Pin and tack (baste) the muslin to the background fabric around its edge. Using your chosen colour of quilting thread, quilt around the petals making sure that they are kept as separate shapes (Fig 3). Make sure your quilting goes right through the muslin too.

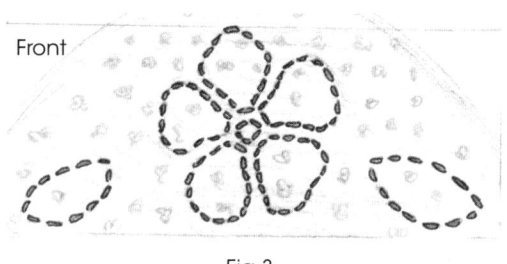

Fig 3

5 Stuff the shapes from the back by easing the stuffing through the warp and weft of the muslin (Fig 4). Do not overstuff. Ease the warp and weft back so that it is in its original place. Remove tacking and trim the muslin, but not too close to the stitches. Once the stuffing is finished, sew the 17in (43.2cm) squares together using ¼in (6mm) seams. Press the seams.

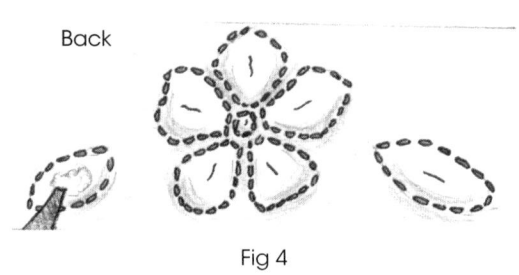

Fig 4

Adding the centre appliqué

6 Use whatever appliqué technique you prefer. I used hand appliqué and template plastic for the leaves, and the appliquéd strips method for the stems. Make the two stems 20in (50.8cm) long. Sew the stems down, covering the seams where the four squares are joined together (Fig 5). Sew them through the cross of seams at the centre so that each stem measures 10in (25.4cm) from the centre along each of the seam lines. (The two stems cross over each other in the centre.)

7 Appliqué two leaves adjacent to each other on either side of each stem, 2in (5.1cm) from the centre point. Appliqué three petals on each end of each stem in a clover leaf pattern, covering the raw edge.

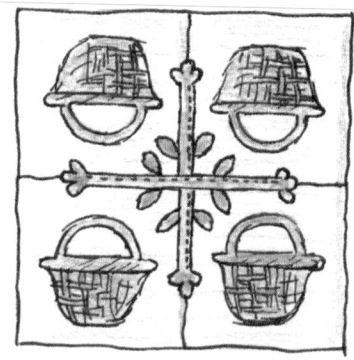

Fig 5

Adding the inner border

8 From background fabric cut two pieces 33½in x 8¼in (85cm x 21cm) and two pieces 49in x 8¼in (85cm x 21cm) – or lengths to fit your quilt. Sew the shorter lengths to the sides of the quilt and the longer pieces to the top and bottom, as described in Adding a Border.

Adding four more baskets

9 Make four more baskets in the same way as before. Attach the handles to the top of each basket.

10 Take four pieces of background fabric each 7in x 4in (17.8cm x 10.2cm) and place the basket and handle over the top of this fabric so the semicircular gap enclosed by the handle is completely covered, with plenty to spare all the way around. Tack (baste) and then sew in place within the semicircle. Trim excess fabric. On the background fabric add the stuffed work as described earlier.

11 Sew the completed baskets in place, overlapping the border and centre panel as shown in Fig 6.

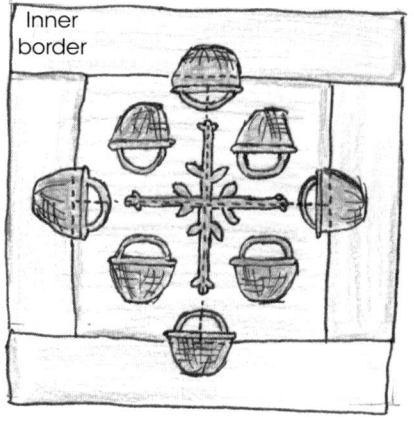

Fig 6

Adding the outer border

14 From the border fabric cut two pieces 49in x 3½in (124.5cm x 8.9cm) and two 54in x 3½in (137.2cm x 8.9cm) or lengths to fit your quilt. Sew the shorter lengths to the sides of the quilt and the longer ones to the top and bottom.

Quilting and binding

15 Press the quilt and follow the instructions in Making a Quilt Sandwich to fix the layers together.

16 Quilt as you choose. I hand quilted using diagonal lines radiating out from the centre, ¾in (1.9cm) apart, with flowers and leaves in the corners and beneath the outer baskets, in the same shape as the stuffed work. I also quilted hares in the borders – see the quilting templates.

17 Finish your quilt with a binding as described in Binding. You will need to join six strips together, each 42in x 2½in (106.7cm x 6.4cm) long.

Adding the corner appliqué

12 Make eight stems 16in (40.6cm) long. Make the leaves and flowers in the same way as the appliqué that covers the seams in the centre. This appliqué covers the seams on the corners. Sew down 9½in (24.1cm) of the stem along the seam to the corner. The extra will flow out from the corner as shown in Fig 7. Cut off the excess stem.

13 Appliqué the petals in a clover leaf pattern. Sew the leaves on the ends near the corners covering raw edges.

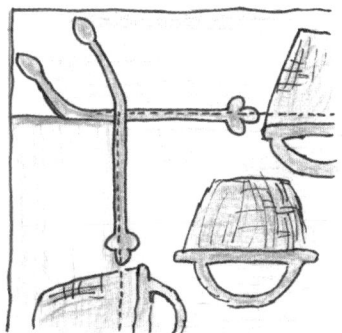

Fig 7

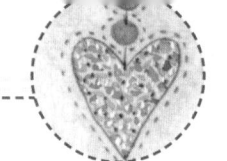

Hanging Heart Decorations

YOU WILL NEED

- Fabric for large heart 10in x 5in (25.4cm x 12.7cm)
- Fabric for medium heart 9in x 4½in (22.9cm 11.4cm)
- Fabric for small heart 6in x 3in (15.2cm x 7.6cm)
- Fabric circles, ten 1½in (3.8cm) squares
- Perle No 8 embroidery cotton 90in (228.6cm) in total
- Buttons, four medium and two small
- Toy stuffing
- Basic kit

Finished size: 21in (53.3cm) total length
Techniques used: using template plastic, simple three-dimensional shapes
Use ¼in (6mm) seams throughout
Templates: Basket on a Shelf

Making the hearts

1 Enlarge the templates to full size. For each heart trace the templates on to template plastic. Cut the shapes out along the drawn line. Fold the heart fabric in half, right sides together. Put the heart plastic template on to the centre of the doubled fabric and draw round it. Machine along the drawn line, leaving a gap unsewn on one side – for the largest heart this is about 2in (5.1cm), less for the smaller hearts. Cut the heart out with a ¼in (6mm) seam allowance around the sewn line. Snip into the raw edge where the fabric curves. Turn the heart out, and stuff with some toy stuffing. Hand sew the gap.

Making the circles

2 For each circle trace the template on to template plastic. Cut the shapes out along the drawn line. Place the circle template in the centre of a 1½in (3.8cm) fabric square and draw round it. Cut out the circle with a ¼in (6mm) seam allowance. Sew a line of tacking (basting) halfway between the drawn line and the raw edge all round. Pull the thread to pull the fabric tight around the plastic. Finger press, remove the plastic and press flat with an iron.

3 Make another circle in the same way. Place the two circles right sides facing outwards, and hand sew together leaving a small gap. Stuff and sew up the gap.

Threading the hearts and circles

4 Decide on the hanging order. Take three strands of perle thread about 30in (76cm). Knot them together at one end. With a large embroidery needle pass these threads through the top of the large heart. Plait the threads for ½in (1.3cm) and make a knot.

5 Thread the perle through the centre of one of the circles from one edge of the stitching to the other. Make another knot close to the circle. Repeat until all circles and hearts are threaded, separated by plaiting. Plait the rest of the perle. Thread it back through the top of the top circle to make a loop of about 3in (7.6cm) and knot the thread. Trim off excess thread.

6 Sew on the buttons. Sew a medium button on either side of the top of the large and medium hearts, to cover the knots. Use the two smaller buttons on the small heart.

You can use this design idea to customize your own decorations, perhaps for small gifts. For example, make single hearts and use circles of bright felt and a pretty button to add further colour and dimension, as shown here.

Under the Greenwood Tree

This group of three pictures has a lovely naïve folk-art quality and is also unusual as the scene flows from one picture to the other. The scenes, in fresh spring colours, are filled with birds flitting about and perched in the trees, with flowers and grasses embroidered beneath them. The design is very versatile – one picture would be equally fine on its own, or you could make pictures one and three as a pair or display all three as a triptych.

The pictures were machine sewn but would also be suitable as a hand project, which would make them very portable. The techniques used include freezer paper appliqué, making appliquéd stems for branches, easy machine stitching and quilting and some fun hand embroidery using thread and silk ribbon.

APPLIQUE FOCUS...

An appliquéd bird can be made up of simple shapes. Adding two stitches for a beak and a French knot eye makes all the difference.

Embroidery by hand or machine is great with appliqué, such as machine stitched grasses and hand stitched silk ribbon flowers.

Appliquéd leaves grouped together create the impression of a tree, especially if using fabrics in different shades of green.

This charming design is so versatile and great fun to make. You can add as much hand and machine embroidery as you like to make it truly original.

Birds in the Trees Pictures

YOU WILL NEED

(For all three pictures)

- Background fabric 37in x 9¾in (94cm x 24.7cm)
- Stabilizer (e.g., Stitch 'n' Tear) 36in x 9¾in (91.4cm x 24.7cm)
- Fabric for tree trunks and branches 21in x 19½in (53.3cm x 49.5cm)
- Scraps of different coloured fabrics for leaves and birds
- Fabric for ground 8½in x 5in (21.6cm x 12.7cm)
- Wadding (batting) 36in x 9¾in (91.4cm x 24.7cm)
- Backing fabric 29in x 15in (73.7cm x 38.1cm)
- Thirty-one tiny buttons
- Embroidery thread and machine quilting thread
- Silk ribbon 2.5mm and 3.5mm wide in assorted colours
- Temporary spray adhesive
- Three wire hangers, each 7½in (19cm) wide
- Basic kit

Finished size: 11½in x 7½in (29.2cm x 19cm) each picture

Techniques used: freezer paper appliqué, appliquéd stems, machine embroidery, hand embroidery, quilting, binding

Use ¼in (6mm) seams throughout

Templates: Birds in the Trees

This pretty design is quite versatile – try stitching just the right-hand and left-hand panels and placing them together for a charming duo.

Preparing the background fabric

1 From background fabric cut three pieces each 12in x 8½in (30.5cm x 21.6cm). Cut three pieces of stabilizer the same size. Spray temporary adhesive on the stabilizer and stick each piece to the back of the background fabric.

Preparing and working the appliqués

2 All three pictures are worked in the same way. I made them one at a time. Enlarge the templates to full size. For a placement guide trace the templates on to greaseproof paper. Trace the tree trunk and the separate bird shapes on to freezer paper. Follow the instructions for the Freezer Paper on Top method. This is used because the pieces will be joined to the background using an ordinary machine stitch.

3 Make the branches in the same way as for stems – see Appliquéd Strips. Find the lengths by measuring the full size template with a tape measure. Allow extra length at either end for turning under at the tip and for tucking under the branch or tree trunk.

4 Make the different leaf shapes using the same freezer paper technique, gathering the raw edge and not sewing right through the paper.

5 Put the greaseproof paper placement guide over the background fabric and position the shapes under the tracing. Pin in place or use a dab from a fabric glue stick. Position and machine round in the following order:
a Small branches, large branches, tree trunk.
b Pink birds – tail, body, wing.
c Yellow birds – tail, wing, body.
d Leaves.

Adding the ground

6 Cut a piece of ground fabric 8¼in x 1½in (21cm x 3.8cm). Along the length of the fabric make a crease line ¼in (6mm) in from the raw edge. Fold the raw edge over making a hem and press well. Place on the background, using the placement guide, and cover the raw edge of the tree trunk with the ground piece. Pin in place at either side.

Sewing the machine embroidery

7 Turn the picture upside down, with the ground at the top. Following the template, embroider the grass, a blade at a time, starting at the right-hand side. Embroider from root to tip, and then back to the root, so each blade is double stitched. When you've finished one blade move horizontally about ¼in (6mm) to the root of the next. Carry on to the left-hand side of the picture. Add embroidered leaves as shown in the template. Stitch the outside of each leaf first and then the veins.

Adding the decoration

8 When all the pieces have been appliquéd tear away the stabilizer from the back of the picture. Hand embroider the birds with a French knot for an eye and two parallel stitches for the beak. Decorate the wings of the flying yellow birds with silk ribbon embroidery. Hand embroider veins on the large leaves, using vertical fly stitch with silk ribbon. Lazy daisy stitch some flowers on the ground with silk ribbon. Add a French knot to the centre of each flower. See Hand Embroidery.

Quilting and binding

9 Press the back of the picture and trim to 11½in x 7½in (29.2cm x 19cm). Follow the instructions in Making a Quilt Sandwich to fix the layers together (I used spray glue), making sure the picture and wadding (batting) is 1½in (3.8cm) below the top of the backing and 1in (2.5cm) away from edge on the other sides. Machine quilt – see instructions for Freehand Quilting.

10 Finish with a binding. Each picture is bound by folding the backing over the wadding and the front of the picture, rather than using separate binding. Starting along one side, fold the excess backing fabric so that the edge butts up to the edge of the picture and wadding and then fold again. Fold a third time, over the raw edge of the picture and wadding by ⅛in (3mm) and stitch down with embroidery thread and a small running stitch. Sew along the whole length from raw edge to raw edge. Repeat on the other side, and then along the bottom.

11 The extra backing fabric at the top is used to make a sleeve for lengths of dowel to be threaded through. Make a crease ⅛in (3mm) in from the raw edge of the backing at the top. Fold the raw edge over and finger press. Stitch in place with a small running stitch. To finish, sew on the tiny buttons randomly on the grasses and at each end of the binding and your pictures are ready to hang.

If you are short on time why not stitch just one picture, which would make a lovely wall decoration or perhaps a cover for a diary or notebook.

Daisy Table Setting

The collection of projects in this chapter was inspired by the naïve quality of folk art, with an imaginary house for little folk, sheltered by large daisies. The idyllic scene is used on a table runner, table mat and coasters to create a lovely table setting which would suit a country kitchen perfectly. The three-storey house design is used again in a three-dimensional form to make two wonderful doorstops filled with marble chips.

Fresh and sunny colours of duck-egg blue, white, cream and egg-yolk yellow are used for the projects. All of the appliqué is done with fusible web, edged with a nicely rustic-looking blanket stitch. There is also some machine stitching and easy quilting and the occasional flurry of hand embroidery to complete the picture.

APPLIQUE FOCUS...

The charming daisies in this collection are appliquéd using fusible web to fuse the shapes securely to the background fabric.

A blanket stitch edging was chosen to outline the appliqué to add to the rustic charm of the little houses and birds.

Extra splashes of colour are brought to the design by the additional of sunny yellow circles dotted between the quilted daisies.

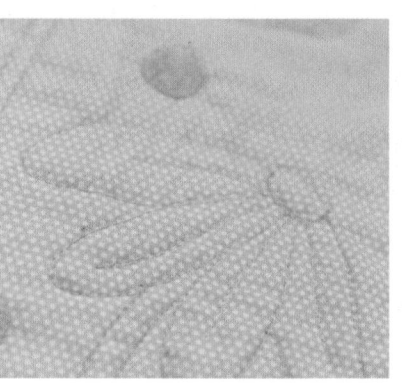

What an utterly charming table setting this is – perfect for afternoon tea in the sunshine. The table runner would make a lovely decoration at any time.

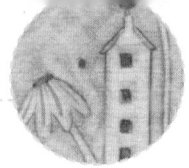

Daisy Table Runner

YOU WILL NEED

- Background fabric 42in x 12½in (106.7cm x 31.8cm)
- Yellow fabric 10in (25.4cm) square for flower centres, birds, some petals, windows and doors
- Scraps of various white/cream fabrics, amounting to 19½in x 28in (49.5cm x 71.1cm) for stems, houses, petals, flower bases, fencing, ground, butterfly and bird wings
- Wadding (batting) 50in x 16in (127cm x 40.6cm)
- Backing fabric 50in x 16in (127cm x 40.6cm)
- Binding fabric 124in x 2½in (315cm x 6.4cm)
- Darning foot for sewing machine if possible
- Basic kit

Finished size: 45½in x 12½in (115.6cm x 31.8cm).
Techniques used: fusible web appliqué, blanket stitch edging, machine quilting, hand embroidery, binding
If using needle-turn appliqué additional fabric will be needed for seam allowances. The runner can be made longer by using a longer piece of fabric and adding more circles and quilting in the centre
Use ¼in (6mm) seams throughout
Templates: Daisy Table Runner

Preparing the background and templates

1 Enlarge the table runner templates to full size and trace the design on to tracing paper or greaseproof paper, making sure that the line on the template is drawn ½in (1.3cm) above the bottom edge of the paper. This will be placed over the background fabric and used as a guide for placing the different pieces and also to protect the iron from the fusible web.

2 Start with a piece of background fabric 42in x 12½in (106.7cm x 31.8cm). Draw a line ¼in (6mm) in from the raw edge at each end. Both ends of the runner are made in the same way (see layout in Fig 1 below). The following instructions are for one end so repeat the process to make the other end.

Appliquéing the stems

3 See detailed instructions in Appliqué using Fusible Web. On the paper side of the fusible web, draw five parallel lines with a ruler 12in (30.5cm) long and ¼in (6mm) apart. Cut the whole area out leaving space around the outer drawn lines. Place the web paper side up, diagonally across the weave of the fabric chosen for the stems and iron on. Cut out the four strips.

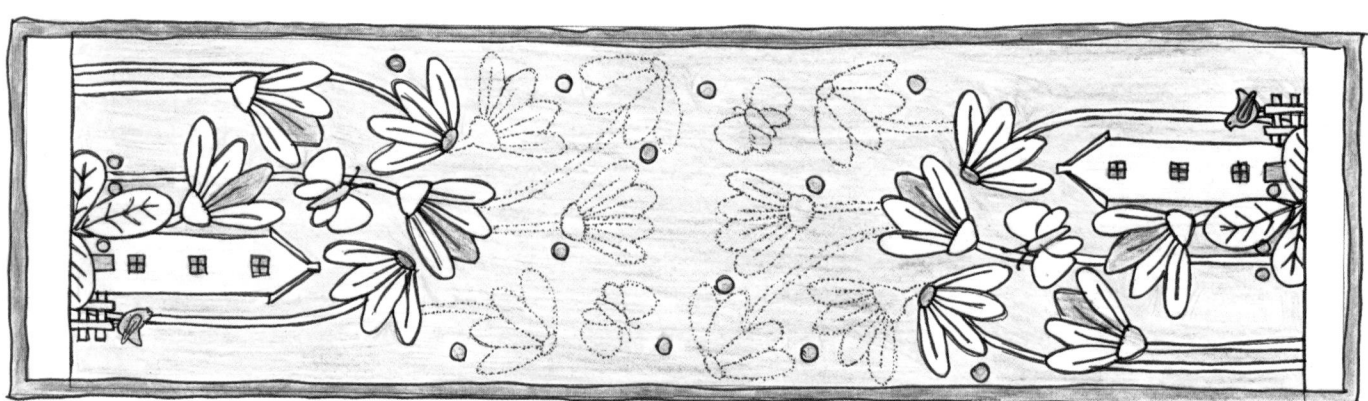

Fig 1 Table runner layout

4 Place the background fabric right side up on the ironing board. Place the tracing paper with the template drawing on top, lining up the base line on the tracing paper with the line on the fabric. Pin the paper to the fabric, making sure it is well aligned and central.

5 For each stem remove the paper side of the fusible web and ease the stem between the tracing paper and the fabric, using the tracing paper template as a placement guide. Cut the stem to size, making sure the end reaches ⅛in (3mm) below the base line with only a small amount of stem under where the petals will go, to avoid stems showing through the cream fabric. Iron the strip down, ironing through the tracing paper. Blanket stitch by hand or machine around the edge of each stem.

Appliquéing the fence
6 Draw two parallel lines 8in (20.3cm) long and ¼in (6mm) apart on the paper side of the fusible web. Cut the area out roughly leaving space around the drawn lines. Iron on to the back of the chosen fence fabric along the grain. Cut into four 2in (5.1cm) strips.

7 Using the tracing paper as a placement guide, ease the fence uprights into position, placing them ⅛in (3mm) below the base line. Iron in place, remove the paper and blanket stitch around the uprights. Add the cross pieces in the same way, making sure there is a small edge that overlaps into the house area.

Appliquéing the house
8 Use fusible web on the fabrics for the house, roof, door and windows. Use the tracing paper template as a guide to placing the shapes. If the edges of one piece touch another, allow a small overlap, e.g., the roof pieces need to be a little bigger to tuck under the house wall. Appliqué the pieces in this order: roof, house, door and windows. Remove the paper and blanket stitch around the shapes.

Appliquéing the flowers, leaves, butterfly and bird
9 There are five flowers, each with four different petal fabrics but not all used in the same order, and some flowers have one yellow petal. Number the petals on the template and on the fusible web to keep track of them. Using the chosen fabrics, prepare all the petals so they are ready to attach to the background. Check the template for which petal to fuse on first, as the order is different for each flower. Fuse the yellow centres and petal bases in place. Add the large leaves at the base of the house, remembering that the leaves should overlap the base line by ⅛in (3mm).

10 Using three different cream/white fabrics prepare the large and small butterfly wings and the body. Fuse the pieces in position in this order: large wings, small wings, body. Fuse the yellow bird's body and then the wing in position. Fuse five little circles in place (but not those in the centre of the runner yet). When all the shapes are fused, remove the paper and then blanket stitch around the shapes. Repeat the process from step 3 to appliqué the other end of the table runner.

Adding the ground and embroidery

11 Place the runner on a cutting mat and trim off excess length. You will need a ¼in (6mm) seam allowance below the base line. Cut two pieces of fabric from your white fabrics each 12½in x 2¾in (31.8cm x 7cm). Using ¼in (6mm) seams, join one of these pieces to one end of the table runner and one to the other end.

12 Hand embroider the bird's wing (backstitch), beak (two little stitches parallel to each other), the eye (French knot) and the butterfly antennae (stem stitch with a French knot on the end) – see Hand Embroidery.

Quilting and binding

13 Using wadding (batting) and backing fabric, prepare for quilting – see Making a Quilt Sandwich. Use the template enlarged earlier to mark the quilting pattern (the dashed lines on the template), using a marker that is water soluble or can be rubbed out. Trace the lines on to your background fabric, using a light box or window. If you have chosen to make your table runner longer, you will need to adapt the quilting pattern appropriately.

14 Machine quilt some lines in yellow on the cream and white flower petals and veins on the leaves. Machine quilt in the ditch (see Quilting in the Ditch) around all the appliqué shapes, keeping the stitches right up against the shape edges. After quilting remove all drawn lines with water or an eraser *before* appliquéing the remaining yellow circles in place. This is because some markers are fixed by the heat of an iron.

15 Cut the excess fabric and wadding so the runner measures 46in x 12½in (116.8cm x 31.8cm). Bind the outside of the runner – you will need a strip 124in x 2½in (315cm x 6.4cm) – see Binding. Your runner is now finished and ready for teatime.

Little House Doorstop

Preparing the templates and background

1 Enlarge the templates to full size. Trace the wall templates on to tracing or greaseproof paper. This will be placed over the background fabric and used as a guide for placing doors and windows and to protect the iron from fusible web.

2 Make a tracing on to freezer paper of the template with the point at each end (front and back walls). Cut out the shape along the drawn line and iron the freezer paper on the back of the background fabric. Cut the shape out with a ½in (1.3cm) seam allowance. Remove the paper.

3 From background fabric cut out two pieces 9in x 4in (22.9cm x 10.2cm) to correspond to the side wall templates. From background fabric cut out two pieces 2in x 2½in (5.1cm x 6.4cm) to correspond to the chimney template.

Working the appliqué

4 Use the tracing paper as a guide for placing the appliqué shapes. Using the technique Appliqué using Fusible Web, appliqué the windows and door to the front and back walls. Appliqué the window to the side walls. Blanket stitch around the edges of the shapes but leave the bottom of the door unsewn.

Joining the roof, wall and chimney

5 Make two tracings on to freezer paper of the roof template. Cut out the shapes along the drawn line and iron them on to the back of the roof fabric. Cut out with a ½in (1.3cm) seam allowance and remove the paper.

6 Put one of the roof pieces and one of the 9in x 4in (22.9cm x 10.2cm) background fabric pieces right sides together. Machine sew together along the 4in (10.2cm) edge of the roof to the background. To get the ½in (1.3cm) seam allowance, draw a line with a ruler on the back of the fabric where the seam will go. Line up the raw edges and then machine along the drawn line.

7 Put the roof right sides together with one of the 2in x 2½in (5.1cm x 6.4cm) chimney pieces. Draw a line for the ½in (1.3cm) seam on the chimney and roof and machine the pieces together along the 2in (5.1cm) width. Repeat with the other roof, wall and chimney.

Applying the wadding

8 For this project there is no need for a backing fabric, as the house pieces are just tacked (basted) on to wadding. Cut out three house shapes in wadding using the house pieces as a guide. Trim the wadding smaller by ½in (1.3cm) all the way round. Spray fabric glue on to the back of the house pieces right up to the edges and then place the wadding centrally on top. Fold the raw edges over the wadding. The glue should be enough to secure the folded fabric but if not tack (baste) down or use a fabric glue stick to hold the edges down.

Working the embroidery and quilting

9 Take the large house piece, fold it in half, (back to back) so the two points meet, and draw a line 1½in (3.8cm) away on either side of the fold. These lines represent the bottom of the walls.

10 Hand or machine embroider along these two drawn lines and then embroider the rambling roses, starting the embroidery at the base of each piece. Look at the templates for details of the pattern. Similarly, embroider the side walls, adding French knots.

11 Quilt the roof. I used machine quilting in a scallop pattern to represent old shingles – see picture below.

Sewing the house together

12 Pin the two pieces right sides together at the point where the roofs meet (see arrows on Fig 1). Starting at the corner at the bottom of the walls, place right sides together and machine stitch along the edge towards the roof.

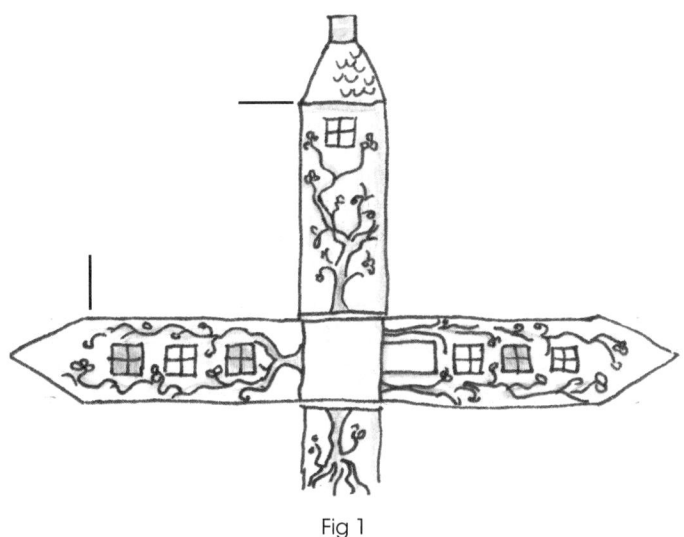

Fig 1

13 Machine sew up to the point where the walls meet the roof and, leaving the machine needle *down* in the fabric, ease the pieces round so that you can machine the roof together (Fig 2). Continue all the way round. Sew up the other sides but for the moment leave the bottom unsewn on one side.

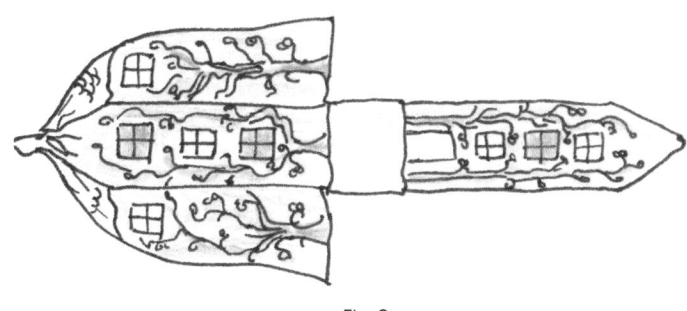

Fig 2

14 Fill the doorstop with small marble chips or clean silver sand. Finish by sewing up the unsewn side with small, neat hand stitches.

Daisy Table Mats and Coasters

YOU WILL NEED

(For four table mats and four coasters)

- Background fabric 39in x 25in (100cm x 63.5cm)
- Yellow fabric 20in x 7in (50.8cm x 17.8cm) for flower centres, birds, some petals, windows and doors
- Scraps of various white/cream fabrics totalling 20in x 29in (50.8cm x 73.7cm) for stems, houses, large petals, flower bases, fencing, ground, butterfly and bird wings
- Wadding (batting) 38in x 35in (96.5cm x 88.9cm)
- Backing fabric 38in x 35in (96.5cm x 88.9cm)
- Binding fabric 330in x 2½in (838.2cm x 6.4cm) – can be cut from a piece 22in x 42in (55.9cm x 106.7cm)
- Darning foot for sewing machine if possible
- Basic kit

Finished size of table mat: 16in x 11½in (40.6cm x 29.2cm).

Finished size of coaster: 5in (12.7cm) square.

Techniques used: fusible web appliqué, blanket stitch edging, machine quilting, hand embroidery, binding
If using needle-turn appliqué additional fabric will be needed for seams
Use ¼in (6mm) seams throughout

Templates: Daisy Table Mats and Coasters

Preparing the background

1 Make all four mats in the same way. The method is similar to the table runner so refer back to those instructions where necessary. Start by cutting a piece of background fabric 16in x 11½in (40.6cm x 29.2cm).

2 Enlarge the template for the mat to full size and trace it on to tracing paper or greaseproof paper.

Working the appliqué and embroidery

3 Follow steps 3–5 of the table runner to make the stem (only one stem is needed here) and fuse it in place, using the tracing paper as a guide to placement. You need a strip about 12in (30.5cm).

4 Using fusible web appliqué as for the table runner, fuse the fence, house, windows, door, flower, butterfly, bird and circles, using the tracing paper as a guide to placement.

5 Hand embroider the bird's wing (backstitch), beak (two little stitches parallel to each other), the eye (a French knot) and the butterfly antennae (stem stitch with a French knot on the end) – see Hand Embroidery for these stitches. Machine embroider or quilt some lines in yellow along the flower petals.

Quilting and binding

6 Using wadding (batting) and backing fabric, prepare the quilt sandwich – see Making a Quilt Sandwich. Use the template, enlarged to full size, to mark out the quilting pattern (shown as dashed lines on the template), using a removeable marker. Draw the lines and machine or hand quilt the flower shapes and in the ditch around all appliqué shapes, as for the table runner.

7 Bind the mat – you will need a strip 60in x 2½in (152.4cm x 6.4cm) for each mat – see Binding.

Daisy Coaster

All four coasters are made in the same way using the same techniques as the table runner and mat. Use the coaster template. Start with a piece of background fabric 5in (12.7cm) square for each coaster. Work the appliqué, making one flower, one bird and one stem about 4in (10.2cm) long. Hand embroider the bird as in step 5 of the table mat. Make a quilt sandwich and machine quilt in the ditch around the appliqués. Trim the coaster to 5in (12.7cm) square and bind it to finish.

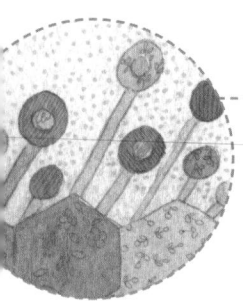

Lollipop Flowers

Fields of flowers are the theme of this chapter in the form of two projects – a very useful sewing bag and a charming small quilt. The bag has a contemporary look with stylized lollipop flowers appliquéd around its circumference. It has lots of room for a sewing kit, with a pincushion in the lid, which is closed by zips.

The quilt has an unusual design and is great fun to stitch. It would make a lovely wall hanging or a table topper. Small hexagons made with English paper piecing create the green centre, with appliquéd lollipop flowers surrounding them. The background is heavily embroidered in French knots, adding texture and detail. A pieced border of triangles, made easy with foundation piecing, is embroidered with stippling, while a third border frames the quilt nicely.

APPLIQUE FOCUS...

The appliquéd flowers couldn't be easier, just simple circles using different colours of fabrics.

A little pincushion with a lollipop flower motif is easily created as an accessory to the sewing bag and fits neatly in the lid.

The appliquéd flowers on the quilt rise up from a bed of hexagons. Dense French knots like pollen give another texture to the work.

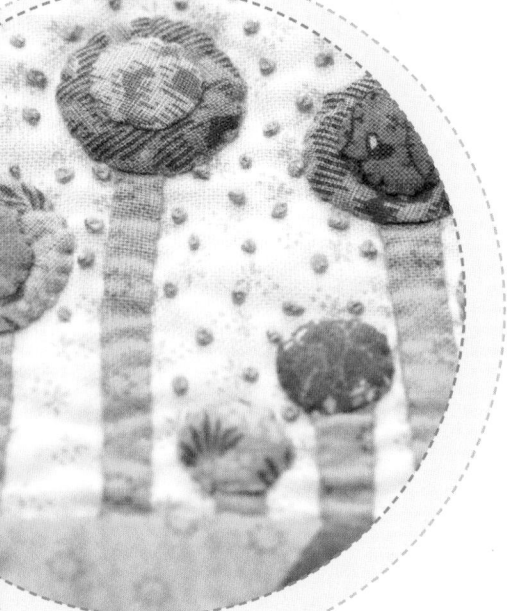

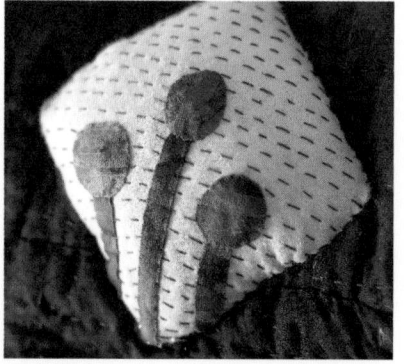

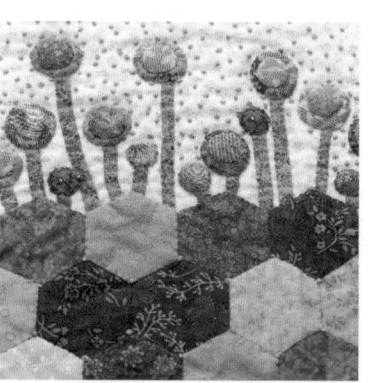

Ultra simple appliquéd circles and strips are really easy to sew and yet create a most charming effect on this small quilt.

Lollipop Flowers Quilt

YOU WILL NEED

- Fabric for background 35in x 19½in (88.9cm x 49.5cm)
- Fabric for inner border 42in x 2in (106.7cm x 5.1cm)
- Scraps of green fabrics for hexagons and stems
- Scraps of different coloured fabrics for flower circles and pieced border
- Fabric for outer border 27in x 8in (68.6cm x 20.3cm)
- Wadding (batting) 31in x 31in (78.7cm x 78.7cm)
- Backing fabric 31in x 31in (78.7cm x 78.7cm)
- Binding fabric 42in x 7½in (106.7cm x 19.1cm)
- Embroidery thread in colours to suit your fabrics
- Machine quilting thread to match fabrics
- Basic kit

Finished size: 28in x 25in (71.1cm x 63.5cm)
Techniques used: English paper piecing, appliquéd stems, appliqué with templates, adding a border, foundation piecing triangle strips, hand embroidery, hand quilting, binding
Use ¼in (6mm) seams throughout
Templates: Lolliopop Flowers Quilt

Making the centre background and hexagons

1 Cut out a piece of background fabric 19½in x 17½in (49.5cm x 44.5cm). Enlarge the templates to full size.

2 Carefully trace the ¾in (1.9cm) hexagon template on to template plastic and cut out the shape. This template is for making paper hexagons which will be used in the paper piecing. Draw around the plastic on to the paper to make a few hexagons and cut them out accurately. Cut a corresponding number of 2in (5.1cm) squares from some of the assorted green scraps.

3 Cut out and piece together sixty hexagons and eight half hexagons using the English Paper Piecing technique. Continue until you have sewn a block of hexagons and half hexagons (see photo, left) Remove the tacking (basting) and papers and press.

4 Place the hexagon block in the middle of the background square and with a water-soluble pen trace around the edge of the hexagons on to the background fabric. Remove the hexagons and put aside. This marking is a guide to where the stems will be sewn.

Adding the stems and flowers

5 Make ⅛in (3mm) wide stems from various green scraps, as described in Appliquéd Strips. Using Fig 1 as a guide, sew the stems in place on the centre background. The base of each stem should be placed about ¼in (6mm) within the line you traced around the hexagons earlier.

6 Make a total of eighty-three small circles and forty-six large circles using the Appliqué using Templates technique. I used metal washers size ¾in (1.9cm) for the large circle and ³/₈in (1cm) for the small. Using Fig 1 as a guide, cover the end of each stem with a large or small circle, using up all the large circles and some of the small. Take the remaining small circles and sew them on top of a contrasting large circle.

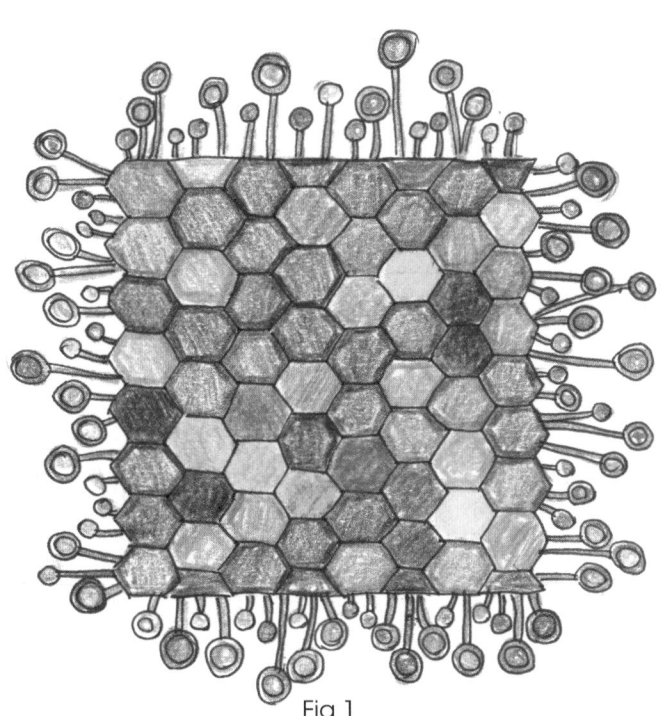

Fig 1

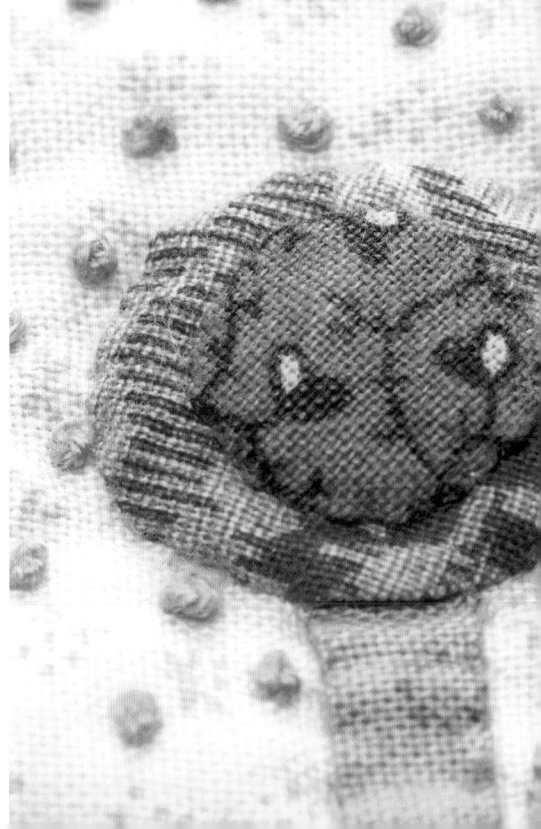

Sewing the hexagons to the background

7 Line up the block of hexagons with the marks on the background fabric. Pin in place and sew, making sure that all the stem ends are covered by the hexagons.

Adding the inner border

8 For the inner border cut two strips 17½in x 1in (44.5cm x 2.5cm) and two strips 20½in x 1in (52.1cm x 2.5cm). Sew on the two shorter strips on opposite sides of the inner background and press. Sew on the two longer strips on the other two sides and press.

Making the foundation pieced border

9 The pieced border consists of thirty-four triangles of background fabric, eight half triangles of background fabric, thirty-eight triangles in assorted colours and four 2½in (6.4cm) squares of background fabric. Using the foundation piecing template, trace the border shape on to a stabilizer (e.g., Stitch 'n' Tear) so that there are two measuring 18½in (47cm) long and two 20½in (52.1cm) long (the red line on the template shows the two sizes).

10 Using the foundation piecing templates make two shapes out of template plastic of the triangle and the half triangle. Cut out all the triangles and half triangles from background fabric, being sure to cut them so the grain of the fabric lines up with the height of the triangles. Similarly, cut out all the triangles from the assorted fabrics. Arrange in a pleasing order, alternating background fabric and assorted fabric. All four sides are made in a similar way. Each side starts and ends with a half triangle of background fabric. The shorter sides have nine coloured triangles and eight background triangles. The longer sides have ten coloured and nine background triangles.

11 Sew the triangles together as described in the technique Foundation Piecing Triangle Strips. Add a 2½in (6.4cm) square of background fabric on to both ends of each of the longer strips and press.

12 Sew the triangle strips to the quilt top, sewing the two shorter sides on first and then the two longer sides with the squares.

Adding the outer border

13 From border fabric cut two 22in x 2in (55.9cm x 5.1cm) strips and two 27in x 2in (68.6cm x 5.1cm). Sew the shorter strips to the sides of the quilt. Sew the longer strips to the top and bottom. Press the work.

Adding the corner appliqué

14 For each corner take a 2in (5.1cm) stem strip, made as before, and sew it diagonally across the corner background square, as shown in Fig 2. There is no need to turn in either end as they will be covered by stems and circles.

15 Cut a 3in (7.6cm) stem strip in a similar way but cut on the bias, diagonally across the fabric so it will curve easily. Sew it in place covering the raw edge at the bottom of the stem, as shown in the diagram. The stem should cover the seam line of the square. Add the large flower circles, then the small ones using the method described earlier. Press the work.

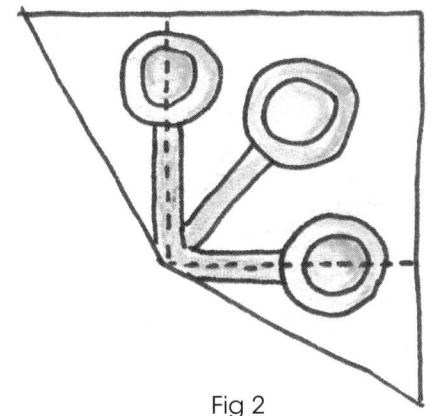

Fig 2

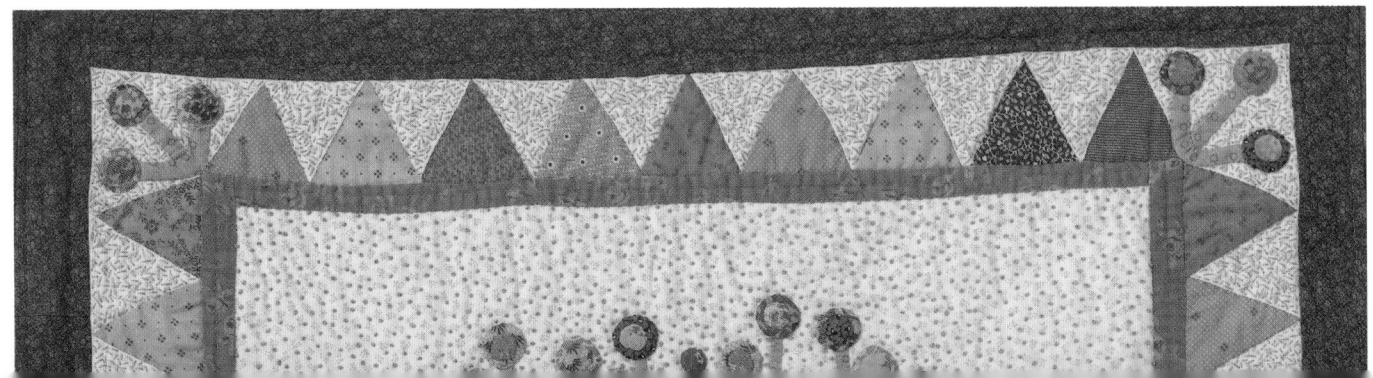

Adding the embroidery

16 Place the quilt on top of the wadding (batting). Smooth everything so that it is flat and tack (baste) across the quilt in a number of places using thread of a contrasting colour. Make sure the tacking goes through the wadding as well.

17 Cover the pale background behind the flowers with French knots. (Think of the French knots as pollen escaping the flowers, being dense in number around the flowers and more spacious as they float up into the air.) Cover the background triangles in the pieced border with seed stitches. I used two strands of embroidery thread for the French knots and the seeding. See Hand Embroidery for stitch diagrams.

Quilting and binding

18 Cut backing fabric 31in (78.7cm) square. Place the completed top and wadding on top of the backing fabric and pin together. To secure the hexagons in place stitch a French knot in each corner right through to the backing. The appliquéd flowers are hand quilted in the ditch, that is, around each flower, including the stem, so that the quilting itself doesn't show, but each shape puffs out.

19 Finish your quilt with a binding as described in Binding.

Flowers Sewing Bag

Making the bag main body

1 Cut out the cream background fabric 19½in x 3½in (49.5cm x 8.9cm). Cut out the green border 19½in x 1in (49.5cm x 2.5cm). Cut out the brown border 19½in x 1¼in (49.5cm x 3.2cm). Cut out the $^1/_8$in (3mm) wide stems as described in Appliquéd Strips.

2 Appliqué the stems to the cream background fabric, using the templates as a guide (enlarged to full size). Make sure that every stem reaches the edge of the fabric. If you prefer, trace the templates on to a fine interfacing (such as Vilene), place it over the background fabric and use it to position the appliqué accurately.

3 Cut out forty-eight 1in (2.5cm) diameter circles, drawing around a $^3/_8$in (1cm) diameter plastic template or washer and cutting out with a ¼in (6mm) margin all around. Fold each circle around the template or washer as described in Appliqué using Templates. Appliqué on a circle, covering the end of each stem.

4 Sew the green and brown borders together. Sew the green border to the background fabric, making sure the raw edges of the stems are covered in the seam allowance.

5 Using the pieces of wadding (batting) and lining, tack (baste) the wadding between the appliquéd fabric and the lining. Quilt lavishly with a contrasting thread.

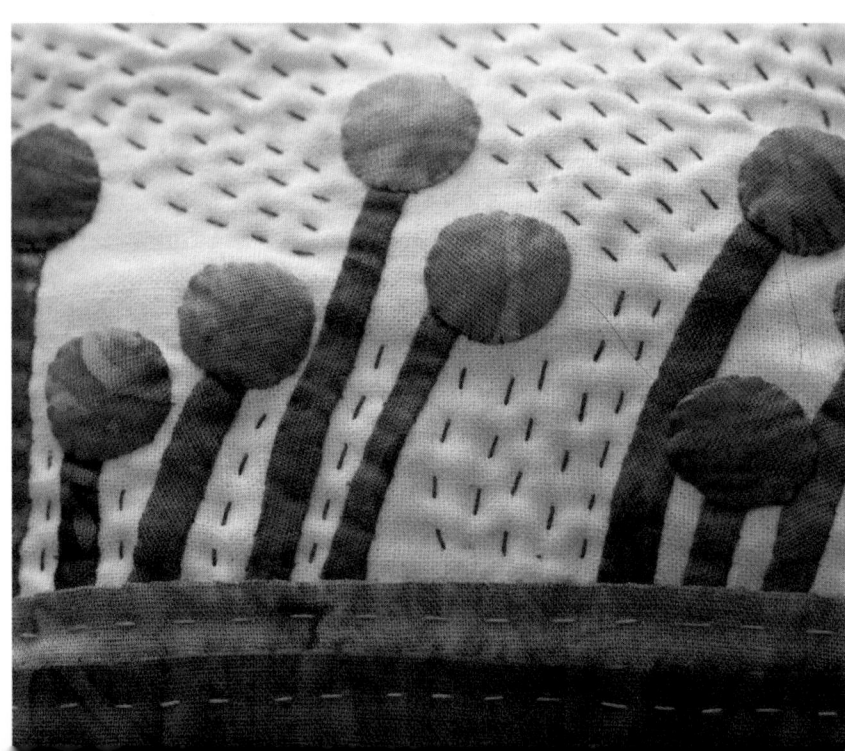

6 Sew the ends together to form a short, fat cylinder. Sew on a piece of lining fabric 4½in x 1¼in (11.4cm x 3.2cm) to cover the seam. Add binding around the top of the cylinder. The binding length needs to be 19½in x 2½in (49.5cm x 6.4cm), cut on the bias and folded double – see Binding.

Adding the bag base

7 Using the template make a plastic template for the base. Draw around the template on to the fabrics for the base, wadding and lining and cut them out.

8 Tack the wadding between the base and lining. Quilt lavishly, this time using a thread that blends with the fabric.

9 Pin the base to the cylinder of the bag and machine or hand sew it on. Add the binding around the base. The binding is the same as that on the main body.

Making the outer lid and handle

10 Draw around the base template on to the fabrics for the background, wadding, and lining and cut them out. Cut out ten stems and circles as before. Appliqué the stems and then the circles on to the background fabric, making sure every stem reaches the end of the lid.

11 Tack the wadding between the background and lining. Quilt lavishly, using a contrasting thread as before.

12 Make the handle by sewing the 4½in x 2½in (11.4cm x 6.4cm) strip along its length, right sides together, into a cylinder. Turn right side out. Quilt it in the same way as the outer lid. Join it to the outer lid by tacking its ends to points halfway along each side of the outer lid (marked on the template).

13 Add the binding around the outer lid (this also secures the handle).

Sewing in the zips

14 Take the outer lid and mark with a pin the point on the lining where one end of the handle joins (i.e., halfway down the side). Pin one side of the left-hand zip around the edge of the outer lid, starting where the pin is, and starting with the open end of the zip, not the joined end. Make sure the zip 'handle' is facing outwards. Hand sew the zip to the lid using double thread (Fig 1). Do the same for the right-hand zip (going the other way round the lid). There should be a gap of about 3in (7.6cm) between the joined ends of the two zips, which will be where the lid is 'hinged' to the bag (Fig 2).

15 Align the lid with the body of bag. Tuck in the zips and pin their other sides to the body of the bag. Hand sew the zips to the inside of the body of the bag (a rather fiddly job).

Adding the inner lid

16 Draw round the base template on to the lining fabric and cut out. Make the inner lid template from template plastic. Draw round it on to wadding and then cut out. If necessary trim the wadding so that it fits within the zips on the lid, covering up the cloth part of the zips.

17 Pin the wadding on to the back of the lining. Fold the raw edge of the lining over the wadding and sew down on itself. To make the inner lid, quilt the lining and wadding together lightly using a blending thread. Pin and then sew the inner lid to the inside of the outer lid, covering the zip by about ¹/₈in (3mm) from the teeth (Fig 3).

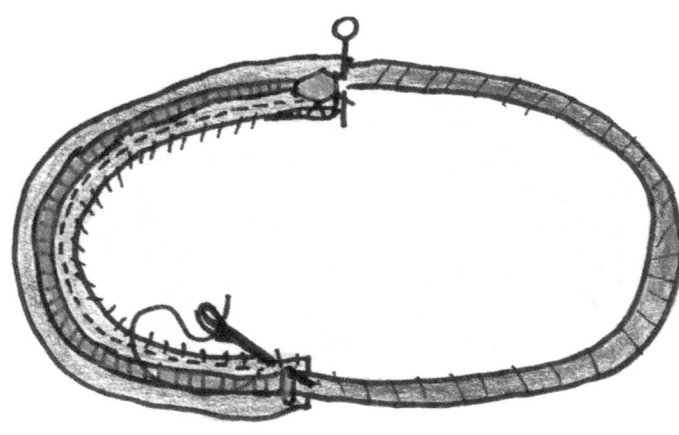

Fig 1

18 Cut out the hinge from lining fabric 4in x 3in (10.2cm x 7.6cm). Fold the hinge in half lengthways, right sides together. Sew it into a cylinder, turn inside out and sew in the raw edges. Sew it across the closed ends of the zips on the inside of the bag, joining the inner lid to the lining of the bag and covering up the gap between the two zips. Neaten the join between the outer lid and body of the bag by sewing the binding on the lid to that on the bag body, just along the hinge line on the outside of the bag.

Making the pincushion

19 Cut out a 7in x 3½in (17.8cm x 8.9cm) piece of background fabric. Fold it in half to make a square. Cut out three stems and three circles. Appliqué the stems and then the circles through both layers of the background fabric, making sure the stems reach the edge (see the template). Tack around the square ¼in (6mm) in from the edge, using strong thread.

20 Take the two squares of greyboard and place them in the middle of the square. Pull the thread, so that the fabric is loosely attached to the board. Poke stuffing between the board and the fabric, until you have a cushion. Pull the thread tight and knot it. Add more rows of tacking to increase the tension.

21 Quilt the pincushion. Hand sew it to the inside of the lid, leaving the board inside, so it looks like a diamond with the flowers pointing upwards.

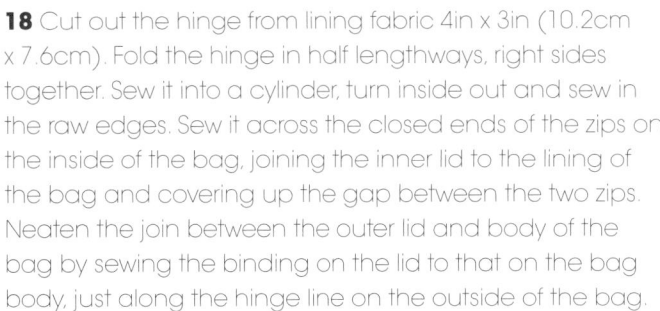

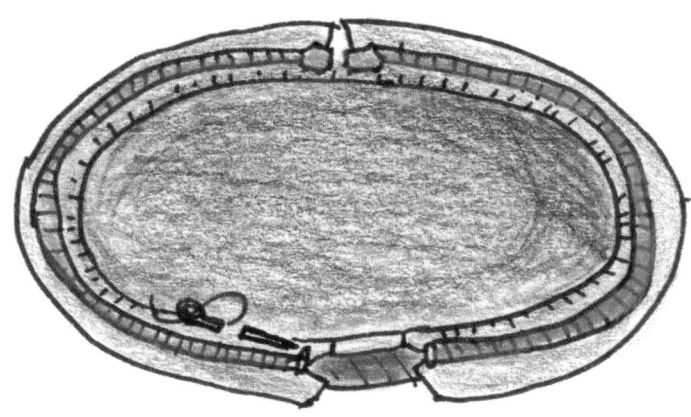

Fig 2

Fig 3

Rose Bouquet

This is such a pretty bag – perfect for a gift. It is heavily quilted in a pattern of interlocking leaves and gives a great opportunity to practise your quilting skills. The bucket-shaped bag has been made in flowery pink and white chintz but you could use a plainer fabric so the quilting would become the main feature. A flower brooch in the same fabric adds a decorative touch.

A second project in this chapter is a useful little pouch, large enough for a mobile phone or pair of glasses. The quilting is simpler, with the main decorative element being a large fabric button. To house a larger phone you can sew the button near the top of the pouch or for a smaller phone fold the top over and place the fabric button further down the pouch.

APPLIQUE FOCUS...

Easy three-dimensional flowers make lovely brooches, especially if sewn with two layers with a button in the centre.

Some hand quilting echoes the shape of the leaves in the fabric and evokes the spirit of whole cloth quilting.

A fabric button is easy to create and makes a functional yet decorative feature – perfect to display a favourite button.

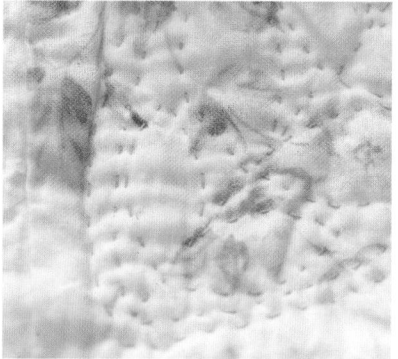

This lovely bag is surprisingly spacious thanks to its bucket shape. It uses a delicate chintz but could be made in any fabric you like. You could make a matching fabric flower for a coat lapel.

Rose Bag

YOU WILL NEED

- Fabric for bag outer 19½in x 28in (49.5cm x 71.1cm)
- Lining fabric 19½in x 21in (49.5cm x 53.3cm)
- Wadding (batting) 19½in x 28in (49.5cm x 71.1cm)
- Fabric for flower brooch 10½in x 7in (26.7cm x 17.8cm)
- Hand quilting thread in a contrasting colour
- Pretty button
- Brooch clasp
- Basic kit

Finished size: 7in (17.8cm) diameter x 8½in (21.6cm) high approx, excluding handles

Techniques used: simple bag making, hand quilting, making a flower brooch

Use ¼in (6mm) seams throughout

Templates: Rose Bag

Cutting out the fabric

1 Cut out the fabric for the outside of the bag as follows. One piece 20in x 12in (50.8cm x 30.5cm) for the sides. One 7in (17.8cm) square for the base. Two pieces each 20½in x 2½in (52.1cm x 6.4cm) for the handle.

Cut the lining fabric as follows. One piece 20in x 9in (50.8cm x 22.9cm) for the sides. One 7in (17.8cm) square for base. One strip 20½in x 1½in (52.1cm x 3.8cm) for binding.

Cut out the wadding (batting) as follows. One piece 20in x 10in (50.8cm x 25.4cm) for the sides. One piece 20½in x 2½in (52.1cm x 6.4cm) for the handle. One 7in square (17.8cm) for the base. Two pieces 3½in (8.9cm) square for the large flower. Two 3in (7.6cm) squares for the medium flower.

Cut the fabric for the flower brooch as follows. Two 3½in (8.9cm) squares for the large flower. Two 3in (7.6cm) squares for the medium flower.

Joining the lining and outside fabric

2 Take the pieces for the outside of the bag sides and the lining and join them by their longest sides to measure 20½in x 20in (52.1cm x 50.8cm). Fold it in half, hiding the seam. Because the outside fabric is bigger than the lining, this means that on one side you will see just the outside fabric and on the other the lining fabric and a 1½in (3.8cm) strip of the outside fabric.

Marking the quilting

3 To create the quilting design enlarge the templates to full size and use them to make plastic templates for the large, medium and small leaf shapes. Using the drawings here as a placement guide, draw around the templates on to the outside fabric with a water-erasable marker, creating the quilting pattern (shown half size in Fig 1). If desired, you could enlarge the diagram by 200% so it is actual size and then trace it.

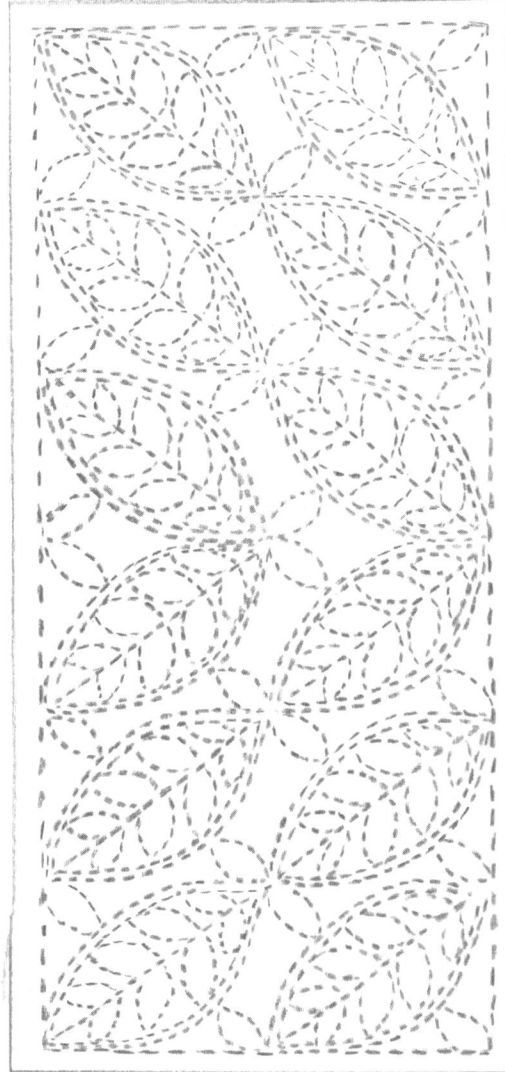

Fig 1

Sewing into a cylinder

4 When you are happy with the marked quilting design, unfold the fabric and place it lining side down. Place the wadding over the lining (it will overlap on to the outside fabric a little) and tack (baste) in place.

5 Fold in half so the wadding is visible at the bottom and back of the outside fabric at the top. Align the raw edges. Machine sew along the length to make a cylinder and sew ¼in (6mm) in from the raw edge. Fold the outside fabric back over the lining and wadding as it was before. Note that the outside fabric overlaps on to the inside of the cylinder a little. There should be three layers: outside fabric with quilt pattern drawn on, wadding and lining fabric.

6 Roughly tack the three layers together. Use a contrasting thread to hand quilt along the drawn lines, starting in the middle and working out to the edges. The piece of outside fabric that extends from the top of the bag can be quilted in straight lines around the cylinder.

Making the bag base

7 Make a plastic template for the circular base 6¾in (17.1cm) in diameter. Draw around this circular template on to the squares of outside fabric, lining fabric and wadding cut out earlier. Cut out these shapes along the drawn line.

8 The quilting on the base is optional if time is short. Using the plastic template made for the medium leaf earlier, draw the quilting pattern (shown half size in Fig 2) on to the right side of the outside fabric using a water-erasable marker. Start with the large leaves that create the diamond shape in the middle and carry on from there (the smaller leaves can be drawn by hand). If desired, you could enlarge the diagram by 200% so it is actual size and then trace it.

9 Make a sandwich of the outside fabric, wadding and lining fabric, with right sides facing outwards. Tack roughly together and then hand or machine quilt along the marked lines.

10 Sew the base to the bag cylinder, using a ¼in (6mm) seam on the outside of the bag. Sew on the binding to cover the seam raw edge. Fold down the top of the bag.

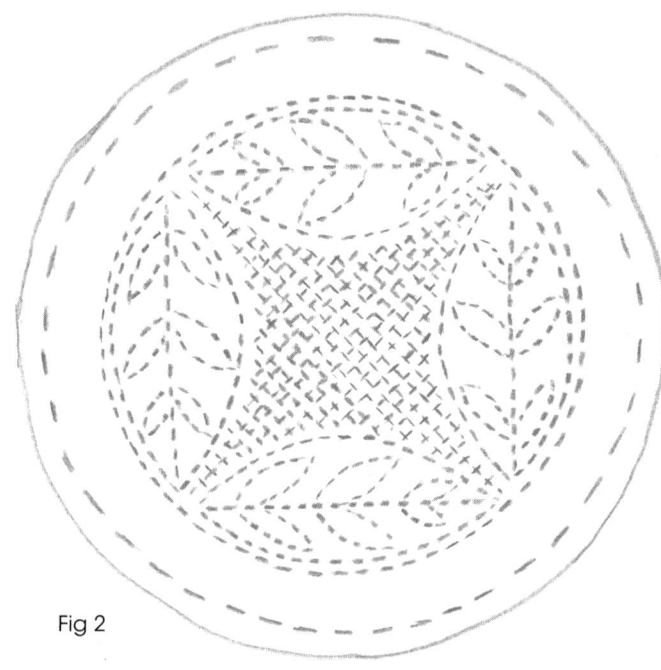

Fig 2

Making the handle

11 Take the two handle strips and place them in this order: wadding, outside fabric face up and then outside fabric face down. Starting at one end, sew along one edge ¼in (6mm) in and continue all around the strips, but leaving one end open. Turn the whole thing inside out, press into shape and sew the open end, tucking the raw edges in.

12 Quilt in straight lines up and down the handle. Sew the handle to opposite sides of the bag, using the pictures as a guide to placement.

Making the brooch

13 The large and medium flowers are made in the same way. Use the flower brooch templates, tracing the shapes on to freezer paper. Cut the paper out along the drawn line. Iron the freezer paper on to the back of one of the 3½in (8.9cm) squares. Draw round the freezer paper on to the fabric with a pencil. Remove the paper.

14 Place the wadding and fabric 3½in (8.9cm) squares in layers as follows: wadding, a second layer of wadding, the fabric right side up and then the fabric right side down (with pencil flower drawing on top). Machine all the way round the flower, leaving no gaps. Snip into the raw edge all the way round. Make a slit through the top layer of the fabric large enough to turn the flower inside out. Turn out, poking out each petal curve and sew up the slit.

15 Make the medium flower in the same way. Place the medium flower on top of the large flower, with the slits sandwiched between the two. Sew a button through all layers and a brooch clasp on the back. Attach to the bag to finish.

Flower Button Pouch

YOU WILL NEED

- Background fabric 17in x 7in (43.2cm x 17.8cm)
- Wadding (batting) 10in x 7in (25.4cm x 17.8cm)
- Fabric for button 7in x 2½in (17.8cm x 6.4cm)
- Pretty button
- Toy stuffing
- Basic kit

Finished size: 6in x 3½in (15.2cm x 8.9cm)

Techniques used: making a fabric button, hand quilting Use ¼in (6mm) seams throughout

Templates: Flower Button Pouch

Cutting out the fabric

1 Both pouches are made in the same way. The body of the pouch is made up of one piece of fabric, which when folded becomes the background and the lining fabric, with wadding (batting) sandwiched between.

From the background fabric cut one piece 14½in x 7in (36.8cm x 17.8cm) for the body of the pouch and one piece 4½in x 1½in (11.4cm x 3.8cm) for the buttonhole.

From the wadding cut one piece 7¼in x 7in (18.4cm x 17.8cm) for the body of the pouch and two 2½in (6.4cm) squares for the button.

For the fabric button cut two 2½in (6.4cm) squares for the body of the flower and one 1½in (3.8cm) square.

Making the buttonhole tag

2 Fold the background piece measuring 4½in x 1½in (11.4cm x 3.8cm) in half along its length, aligning the edges. Machine sew one end and all the way along the length ⅛in (3mm) in from the raw edge. Leave the other end open.

3 Turn inside out and press. Cut off the sewn end. Fold in half along the length once more, align the edge and hand sew the two edges together to made a narrow strip.

Making the body of the pouch

4 Fold the background fabric in half, right sides together so that it measures 7¼in x 7in (18.4cm x 17.8cm) and press. Open the fold and line up a ruler so that the edge is 1¼in (3.2cm) to the right of the fold. Place the buttonhole tag up against the ruler. Pin both ends of the tag into a loop with the raw ends sticking slightly above the raw edge of the background fabric (see Fig 1).

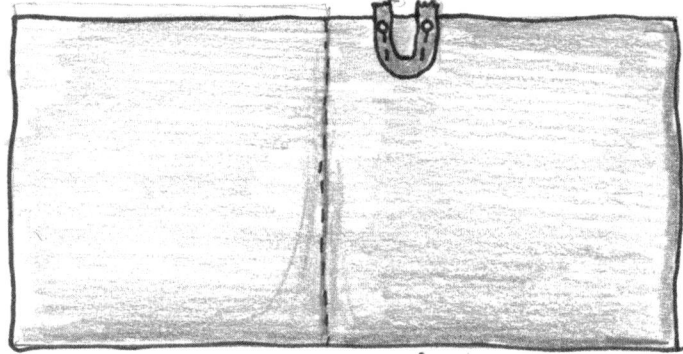

Fig 1

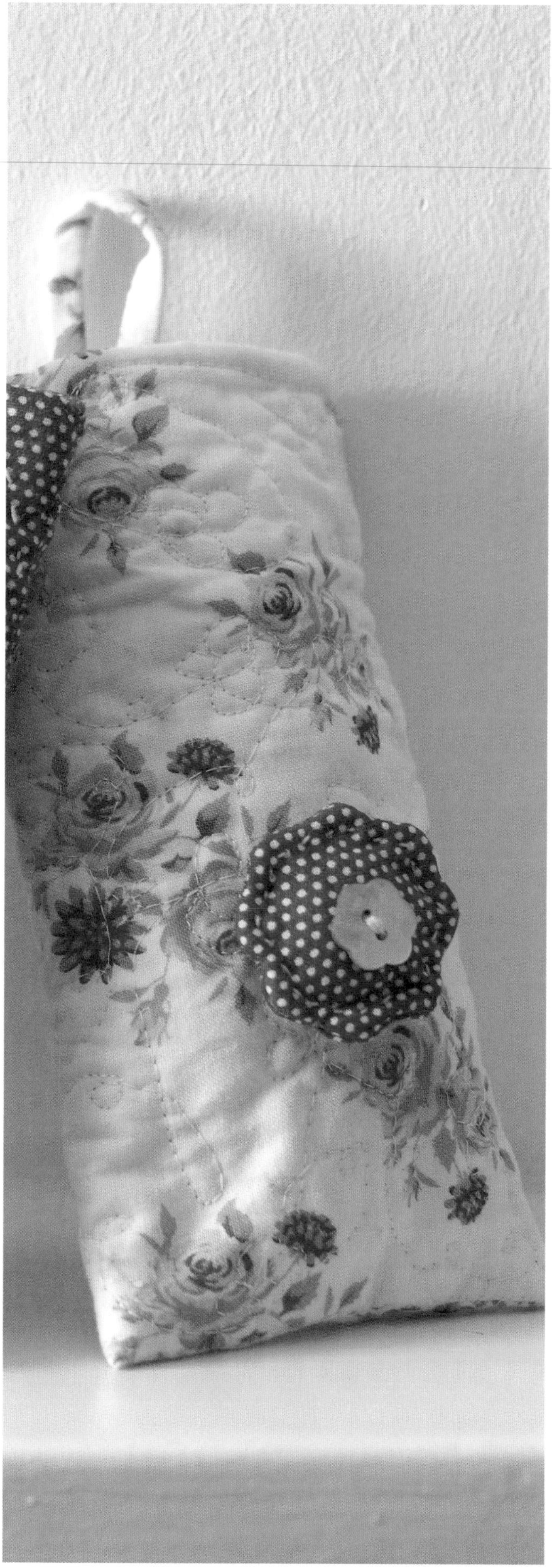

5 Fold the background fabric again as before. Place on top of the 7¼in x 7in (18.4cm x 17.8cm) piece of wadding. Pin the three layers together as follows: wadding, folded fabric (face up), buttonhole tag and then the folded fabric (face down). Machine sew around the four sides of the rectangle, leaving a gap of 2in (5.1cm) on one of the sides. Turn the whole thing inside out through the gap, poking out the corners and then hand sew the gap closed. Quilt as you wish.

Making the fabric button

6 Trace the template of the flower on to freezer paper. Cut the paper out along the drawn line. Iron the flower freezer paper on to the back of one of the 2½in (6.4cm) squares, in the centre. Carefully draw round the freezer paper on to the fabric with a pencil and remove the freezer paper.

7 Place the wadding and 2½in (6.4cm) squares of fabric in layers as follows: wadding, another layer of wadding, the fabric right side up and then the fabric right side down (with pencil flower drawing on top). Machine all the way round the flower, leaving no gaps. Snip into the raw edge all the way round. Make a slit through the top layer of the fabric large enough to turn the flower inside out. Turn inside out, poking out each curve of the flower petals.

8 Using the 1½in (3.8cm) square, make a circle using the circle template and then make an appliqué circle following the instructions in Appliqué using Templates using template plastic and a washer or coin. Sew the appliqué circle over the slit. Stuff the circle with some toy stuffing before sewing all the way round. The circle side of the button should be at the back.

9 Quilt round the fabric button and sew a pretty button on top of the flower. Depending on the size of your mobile phone or glasses sew the button at the top of the pouch or further down.

Sewing up the pouch

10 Finish the pouch by folding it in half with the buttonhole tag at the top and the button facing outwards. Align the edges and hand sew the pouch together.

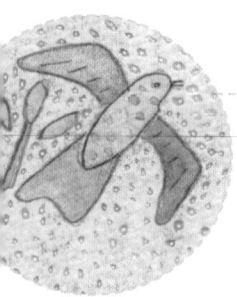

Birds of a Feather

The main project in this chapter is a gorgeous quilt filled with felt birds, flowers and leaves appliquéd with fusible web on to brushed cotton. The colouring is exciting, with flashes of bright blues, pinks and yellows bringing extra zing. Additional detail is achieved with needle felting, machine embroidery and machine quilting in a doodling pattern of tiny flowers. The quilt uses seven different blocks, which are repeated in a reversed layout to create a visually stunning design.

Two colourful felt mats are also included in this chapter, in different colourways, featuring a plump felt appliquéd bird nestling among flowers and leaves, in a circle surrounded by petals. The mat can be used flat or be hung on a wall as a decoration. The appliqué is made easy with fusible web edged with blanket stitch, while hand embroidery embellishes the whole mat.

APPLIQUE FOCUS...

The birds on the quilt are made with simple appliqué shapes, with needle felting bringing extra detailing and spots of colour.

The appliqué is given even more of a folk-art look with a blanket stitched edging. Appliquéd circles of felt are an alternative to felting.

Random machine quilting in toning thread and a tiny flower pattern meanders over the quilt, bringing the whole design together.

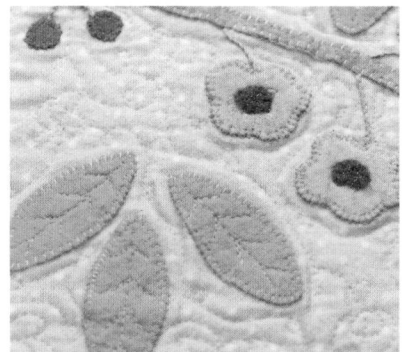

This fabulous quilt with its lovely colouring is simpler to make than it looks. It is a real pleasure to create and is sure to attract much admiration.

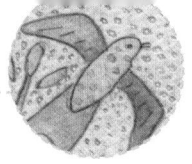

Feathered Friends Quilt

YOU WILL NEED

- Brushed cotton fabric for background and binding 106in x 42in (270cm x 106.7cm)
- Wool felt pieces (see also * below): stems 35in x 12in (88.9cm x 30.5cm); leaves 35in x 12in (88.9cm x 30.5cm); flowers 18in x 12in (45.7cm x 30.5cm); scraps of different colours for birds' bodies, wings, tails (the largest pieces being 6in/15.2cm square); scraps of felt for berries
- Backing fabric 60in x 53in (152.4cm x 134.6cm)
- Wadding (batting) 60in x 53in (152.4cm x 134.6cm)
- Small amounts of wool tops for felting
- Needle felting mat
- Pen-style needle felting tool
- Embroidery threads to match fabrics
- Basic kit

Finished size: 55in x 48in (139.7cm x 121.9cm)

Techniques used: appliqué using fusible web, needle felting, machine embroidery, hand embroidery, adding a border, quilting, binding
* The felt measurements are for unwashed felt. If pre-washing, add 20–30% to measurements, as felt shrinks by an unpredictable amount. Needle felting could be replaced with appliquéd circles if preferred
Use ¼in (6mm) seams throughout
Templates: Feathered Friends Quilt

Preparing the background fabric

1 The blocks are arranged in four rows, and each block shape is used once in the top half of the quilt and again in the bottom half to create visual variety. In the top half of the quilt the bird motifs are reversed (so the final appliqué will look like the template drawing) but in the bottom it is not – see Fig 1. Cut the background fabric as follows:
Block 1 and 1 reversed 12in x 16½in (30.5cm x 41.9cm).
Block 2 and 2 reversed 12in x 12in (30.5cm x 30.5cm).
Block 3 and 3 reversed 6½in x 11½in (16.5cm x 29.2cm).
Block 4 and 4 reversed 6in x 11½in (15.2cm x 29.2cm).
Block 5 and 5 reversed 12in x 11in (30.5cm x 27.9cm).
Block 6 and 6 reversed 12in x 16½in (30.5cm x 41.9cm).
Block 7 and 7 reversed 12in x 12½in (30.5cm x 31.8cm).

Appliquéing the blocks

2 All of the blocks are made in the same way. Start by drawing on greaseproof paper the rectangle or square of the cut dimensions of the relevant block (see Fig 2). Enlarge all the templates to full size. Remember that the templates show the finished design. Trace the template for the appliqué inside the shapes.

3 The appliquéd shapes are bonded on to the brushed cotton using fusible web – see Appliqué using Fusible Web. Using the paper drawing as a guide, bond the different pieces on to the relevant fabrics. Generally, bond the branch on first. If there is a separate tail and/or wings that look as if they go under the body, then bond these next. Follow with the bird's body and the other pieces. When everything is in place, machine around the edges using your favourite stitch, such as blanket stitch if you have it, or zigzag or satin stitch.

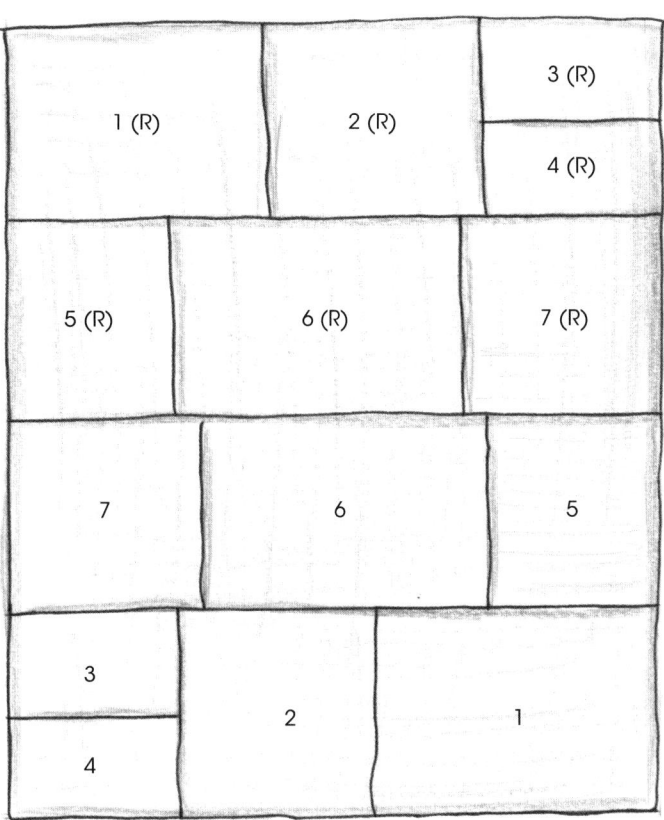

Fig 1
R = reversed block

Fig 2

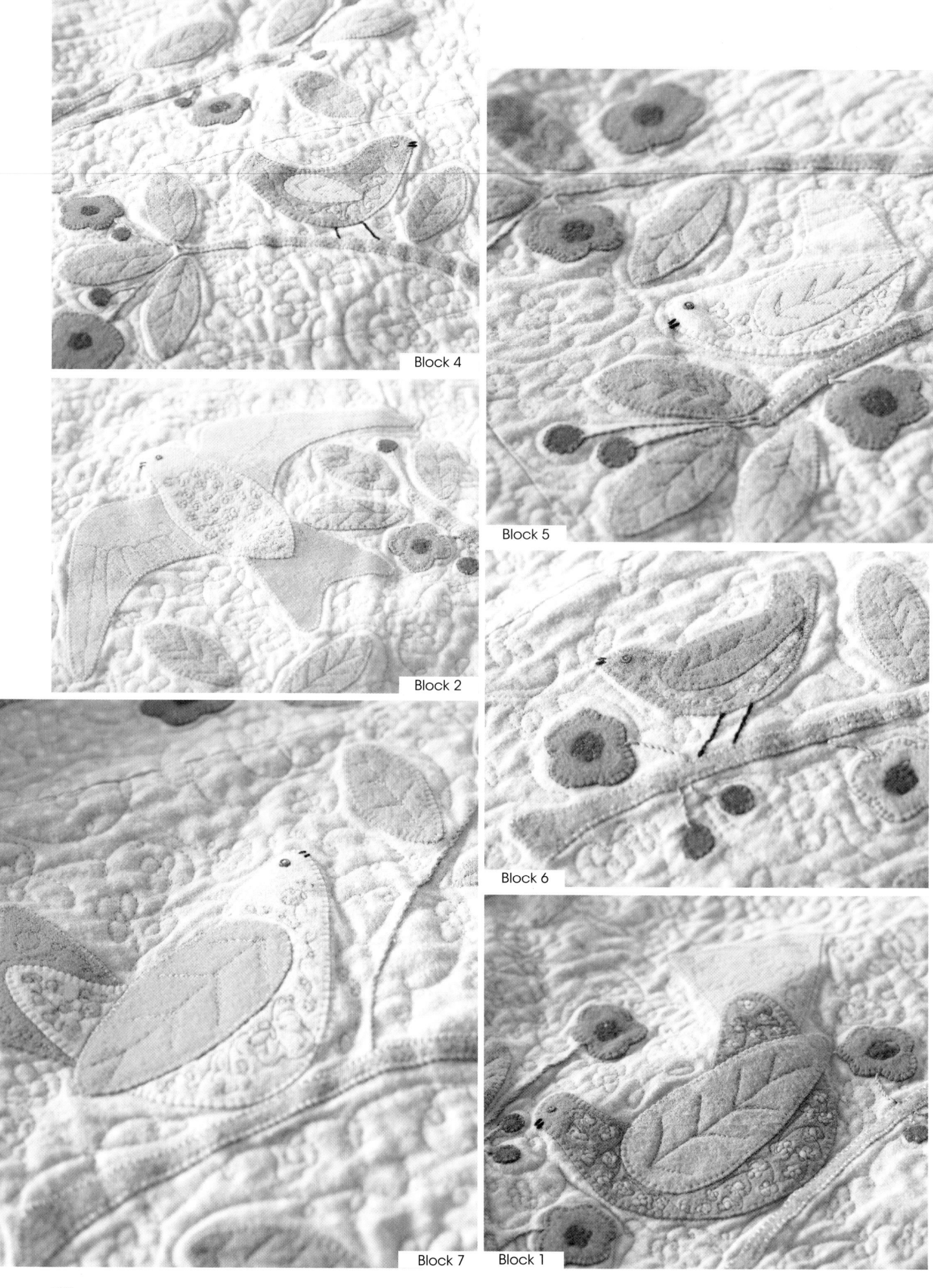

Block 4

Block 5

Block 2

Block 6

Block 7　　Block 1

Adding the decoration

4 When all the pieces have been appliquéd, decorate each bird's breast with needle felting – see Needle Felting. Alternatively, bond on small circles of felt. Add small circles on the breasts and at flower centres. See the Felt Mats overleaf for other ideas on decoration.

5 To keep the needle felting in place machine embroider over the areas – see Machine Embroidery. Add detail on the birds' wings and tails. The wings on top of the bodies have the same pattern as the leaves, a machine representation of vertical fly stitch, but you could work it by hand – see Hand Embroidery. Each bird has two stitches parallel to each other for a beak and a tiny button for an eye. A French knot could replace the button. Stem stitch the berries to the branches. Use two strands of thread for hand embroidery.

Joining the blocks

6 Join the blocks together using Fig 2 as a guide. Take care not to confuse each block with its reversed version.

Adding the border and appliqué

7 Cut two strips of background fabric each 39in x 5in (99.1cm x 12.7cm) and machine sew them to the bottom and top of the quilt. Press the seams. Cut two strips each 55½in x 5in (141cm x 12.7cm) and sew them to the sides. See Adding a Border.

8 The appliqué in the border is a branch with three leaves and two berries that is repeated in a mirror image on all four sides of the quilt. Draw a rectangle 24in x 4½in (61cm x 11.4cm) on to greaseproof paper and within the shape make a tracing of the branch, leaves and berries. Use this tracing as a guide to bond and appliqué the pieces on to the border in the same way as before.

Quilting and binding

9 Press the quilt and follow the instructions in Making a Quilt Sandwich to fix the layers together. Quilt using a freehand pattern of your choice.

10 Finish your quilt with a binding as described in Binding. You will need to join five strips of background fabric together, each 42in x 2½in (106.7cm x 6.3cm) long.

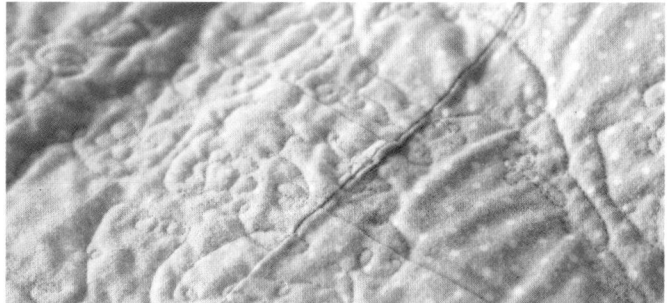

Bird Mats

YOU WILL NEED

(For one mat)
- Background fabric 18in x 12in (45.7cm x 30.5cm)
- Scraps of coloured felt
- Embroidery thread to suit your fabrics
- Tiny button for bird's eye
- Pretty button to hang the mat
- Basic kit

Finished size: 9¾in (24.8cm) in diameter
Techniques used: appliqué using fusible web, appliqué using freezer paper, appliqué using templates, hand embroidery
Use ¼in (6mm) seams throughout
Templates: Bird Mat

Preparing the background and circle edging

1 Both mats are made in the same way. Enlarge the templates to full size. Using the template trace the circle on to freezer paper. Cut out and iron on to the felt. Cut out the circle up against the paper. Peel the paper off and make another circle.

2 Using the template trace one of the outer petals on to template plastic, making the shape a ¼in (6mm) longer as the petals need to tuck under the circle. Cut the plastic out. Trace round this on to fusible web nineteen times. Roughly cut out the whole section of the traced fusible web and iron it on to the felt. Cut out the petals individually. Peel off the paper backing and iron them on to the same coloured felt to make a double thickness. Cut them out again.

Working the appliqué

3 Using the template trace the whole design on to greaseproof paper so the tracing is drawn ½in (1.3cm) above the bottom of the paper. This will be used as a guide for placing the different pieces and to protect the iron from the web. Using this tracing, copy the different shapes on to the fusible web, grouping together the shapes that you want to be the same coloured felt. Make the tail a little bigger where the wing meets the body as the wing will tuck under the bird a little. See Appliqué using Fusible Web. Cut the shapes out roughly and then iron them on to the chosen felts. Cut the shapes out along the drawn line.

4 Place the circle on top of greaseproof paper on the ironing board. Place the greaseproof drawing over the top, aligned with the circle. Pin at the top of the paper to keep in place. Position the shapes under the paper, starting with the stem, and iron in place. Position the bird, starting with the tail, then the body and wing. Iron through the greaseproof. The iron needs to be quite hot for the fusible web to work but take care as some felts may not stand too high a temperature – experiment on a scrap first.

5 Blanket stitch round all the shapes. Work vertical fly stitch on the leaves and wing. Add back stitch detail on the bird's body and wing. Stem stitch the tendril. Add French knots to flower centres. See Hand Embroidery for working these stitches.

Constructing the mat

6 Place the second circle cut out earlier on the table with the double thickness petals evenly around the edge of the circle so the flat ends overlap the circle by ¼in (6mm) – line up a ruler ¼in (6mm) in from the flat end of the petal and place a pencil mark on either edge. Line these marks up with the circle edge. Alternatively, place the greaseproof paper over the circle to get the spacing even. Dab a little glue where the ¼in (6mm) overlaps the circle.

7 Place the appliquéd circle on top, covering the flat ends of the petals and aligning both circles. Pin in place. Turn over to the back and sew the circle to the petals with over stitch. Turn to the front and blanket stitch around the circle.

Finishing off

8 Blanket stitch round all the petals and work vertical fly stitch in the centres. To hang the mat up, cut a strip of felt the desired length and ½in (1.3cm) wide. Sew a button on the back of the mat, cut a slit for a buttonhole at one end and place over the button.

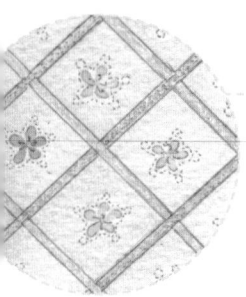

Buttercup, Buttercup

This lovely quilt is hand appliquéd with flowers within square blocks, which are machine pieced and arranged in a diagonal 'on point' format. Appliquéd strips arranged in a woven pattern in two different fabrics cover the seams. A border frames the blocks with entwined stems, flowers and leaves, the stem changing tone as it winds around the quilt. The flowers are in a variety of different yellows with a green centre and are embroidered with variegated thread.

This chapter also has two wonderfully plump, gathered cushions in two different designs of three-dimensional buttercup flowers and leaves combined with hand embroidery. The drawstrings have sweet little flowers at the ends.

APPLIQUE FOCUS...

At the centre of each quilt block is a simplified daisy flower, decorated with hand embroidery and with the shape echoed by quilting.

In each corner the appliquéd stem knots around itself attractively, sprouting a cluster of daisy buds and leaves.

Three-dimensional appliqué flowers are easy to create and make a pretty detail, especially on the drawstrings.

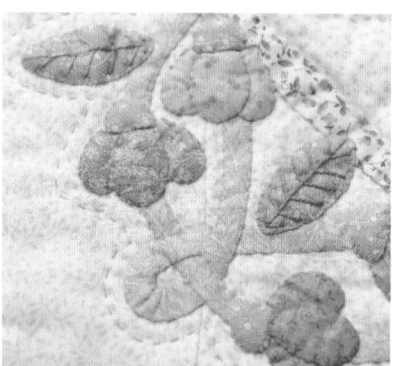

Fresh and spring-like, this buttercup-inspired quilt will look pretty in any room and could be made in a bigger size quite easily.

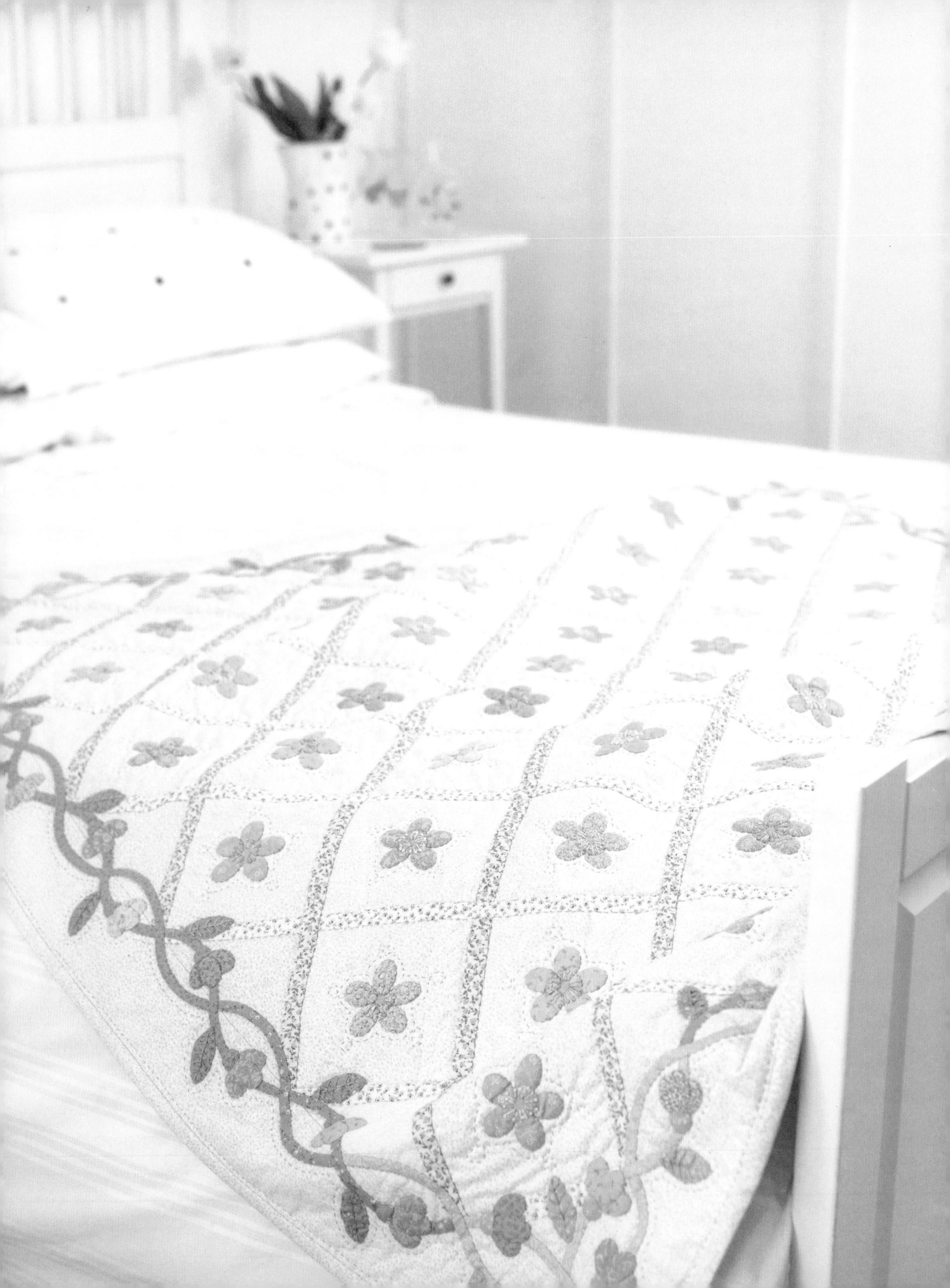

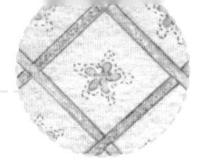

Buttercup Quilt

YOU WILL NEED

- Different cream fabrics for background totalling 118in x 42in (300cm x 106.7cm)
- Different yellow fabrics for flowers totalling 39½in x 42in (100cm x 106.7cm)
- Scraps of fabrics for flower centres
- Fabric for warp strips 42in x 19½in (106.7cm x 49.5cm)
- Fabric for weft strips 42in x 19½in (106.7cm x 49.5cm)
- Three different fabrics (light, medium and dark) for stems totalling 42in x 19½in (106.7cm x 49.5cm)
- Three different fabrics for leaves and flower bases totalling 21in x 19½in (53.3cm x 49.5cm)
- Backing fabric 58in x 58in (147.3cm x 147.3cm)
- Wadding (batting) 58in x 58in (147.3cm x 147.3cm)
- Binding fabric 42in x 14in (106.7cm x 35.6cm)
- Embroidery thread in colours to suit your fabrics
- Hand quilting threads in green and a colour to tone with fabrics
- Basic kit

Finished size: 51in x 51in (129.5cm x 129.5cm)

Techniques used: appliqué using templates, hand embroidery, simple machine piecing, adding a border, appliquéd strips, hand quilting, binding

Use ¼in (6mm) seams throughout

Templates: Buttercup Quilt

Preparing the background fabric

1 The quilt is made up of sixty-one squares, all made in the same way but with varying background fabrics and different yellows. Cut the 6in (15.2cm) square blocks out as you go along so that you get a good feel for the balance of fabrics. I also cut the border fabric when I need to add it, to allow me to change the fabric, or if the measurements turn out different from planned.

Preparing the flower centres

2 Each flower at the centre of the 6in (15.2cm) square has five petals with a circle of green fabric under the petals. Enlarge the templates to full size and use them to trace the petal shape and flower centre on to template plastic. Cut out along the drawn line and use them to replicate the petals and flower centres throughout the project.

3 Draw around the flower centre on to the back of your fabric and cut them out along the drawn line. Each centre is placed under the petals as it is and the petals cover the raw edge. Use the plastic petal template to make the petals as described in Appliqué using Templates. Cut a piece of template plastic 6in (15.2cm) square. Place the plastic over the template drawings of the square block. (In the drawing the square shows the finished size, not the raw edge size, so the plastic will overhang slightly.) Trace the flower shape on to the plastic. Cut a hole in the plastic the shape and position of the flower. With a bit of tape, mark one corner of the plastic. This will help you place the petals in the right place on all the squares, and the tape will help you to use it the same way round every time.

Appliquéing the petals

4 For each of the sixty-one square blocks cut out a 6in (15.2cm) square of background fabric. Place it right side up and mark the top right corner with a water-soluble marker. Put the plastic placing template on top of the square, matching up the marks so that they are at the same corner. While the plastic is on the fabric place the green circle in the middle and then place the petals in the slots made by the plastic. Pin the petals in place. Remove the placing template and sew the petals down.

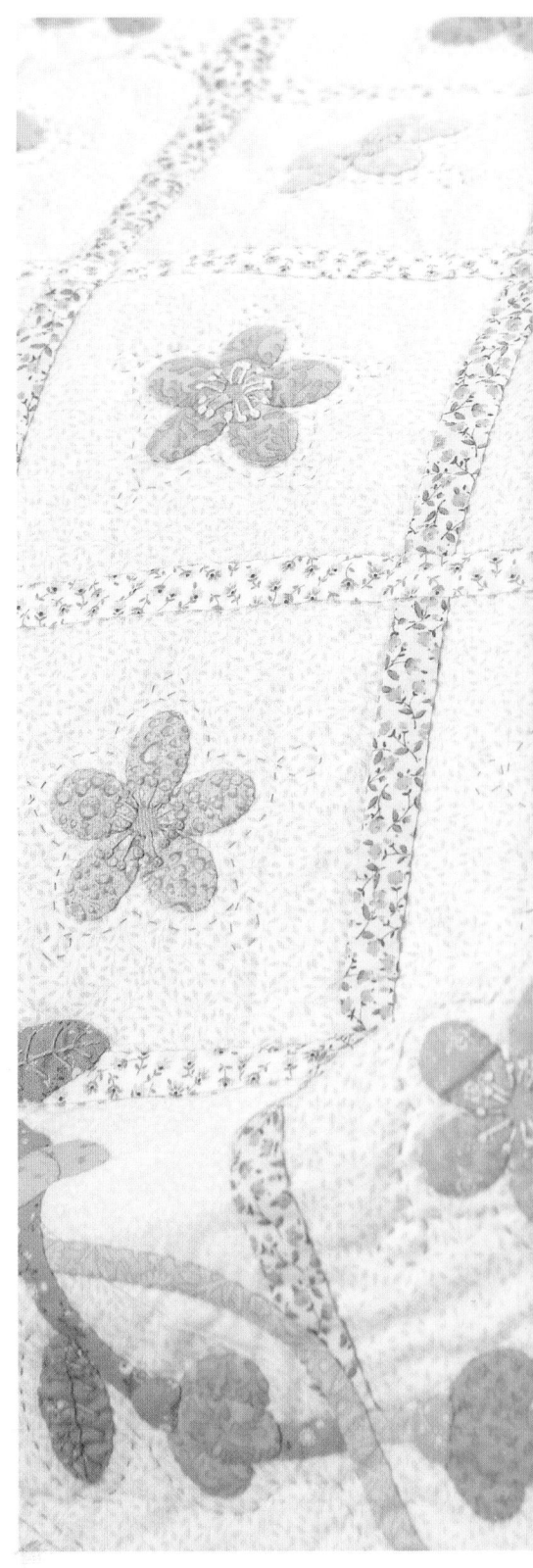

Adding the embroidery

5 In the flower centre embroider some stamens, each a single long stitch with a French knot at the end (see flower detail picture below).

Joining the blocks

6 When all sixty-one squares are appliquéd place them on the floor and arrange them in a pleasing way. Make sure that each square has its mark at the top right corner. The squares will be sewn together in diagonal rows, so they are on the point. Along the edge there will be inset triangles.

7 From background fabric, cut five 8¾in (22.2cm) squares. Cut each across both diagonals for a total of twenty triangles (inset triangles). Starting in one corner, sew rows of squares together as shown in Fig 1, taking care to get the triangles the right way round. Row 1 starts with one square with triangles on opposite sides, building up to eleven squares in Row 6. The triangles then change direction and mirror image those of the previous rows. Sew the rows together in order – the first row to the second row, second row to third row, and so on.

8 Four corner triangles are now needed. Cut a 7in (17.8cm) square from background fabric and cut across both the diagonals to make four triangles. Machine sew them to each of the four corners of the quilt. Remove the marks made on the blocks at this stage if desired.

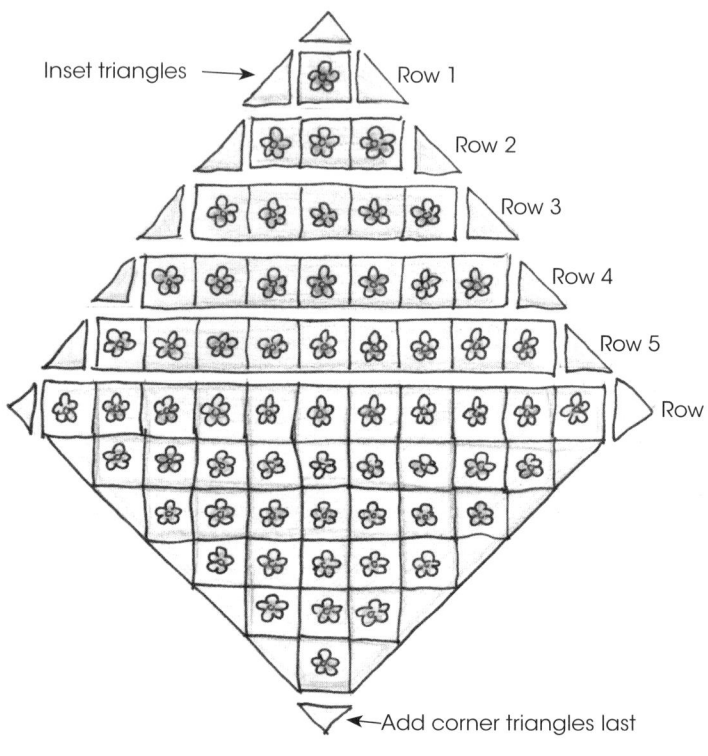

Fig 1

Adding the warps and wefts

9 Press the quilt top and make sure the seams on the back are flat. The seams between the square blocks will be covered by appliqué strips which overlap each other in a woven pattern. One fabric is used for the 'warp' (vertical) strips and another for the 'weft' (horizontal) ones. Choose which fabric is going to be the warp and cut the fabric along the width so that you have a series of strips 42in (106.7cm) long and ½in (1.3cm) wide when turned under. See Appliquéd Strips. Make the weft strips in the same way. Keep the warps and wefts in separate piles.

10 The warps are parallel to each other. Place the quilt top on a table. With a water-soluble marker mark the quilt now and again ¼in (6mm) from the seams. This will help when sewing the strips in place. The warps and wefts overlap at the corners of the squares. Work out which of these overlaps will have the warp going *under* the weft, and mark those corners with a tag of thread. Where these tags are, two warps can be joined together without being seen. Roughly pin the warps on the quilt following the small guidance marks (Fig 2). If a strip is not long enough take it back to the nearest tag and join a new strip there. The two ends butt up against each other but it's best not to cut the excess strip until warps and wefts are sewn down as the strips shrink in the sewing. When you are happy with the placing, pin more thoroughly.

11 Sew along both sides of the strip stopping a good ¼in (6mm) either side of the seam where the weft will be going under the warp. Sew a double stitch and pass the thread to the back. Pass it to ¼in (6mm) from the seam, do another double stitch and then carry on. This creates a gap for the weft to pass through. Continue until all the warps are sewn in place.

12 Now sew on the wefts, woven at right angles to the warps. Thread the wefts through the gaps, using a large bodkin or similar, pinning in place (Fig 3). If a strip is not long enough take it back to the nearest gap and join a new strip there. Sew both sides of the strip, easing the strip as you go. Press the work.

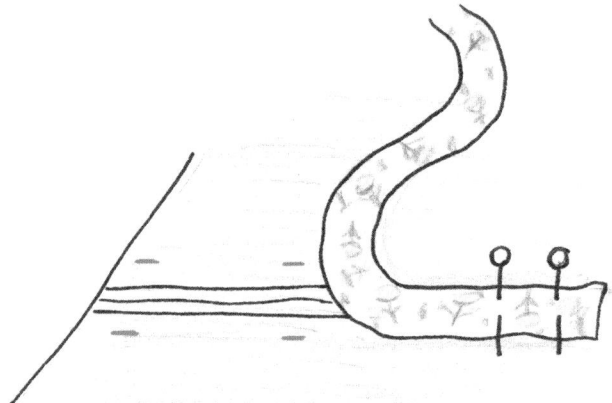

Fig 2

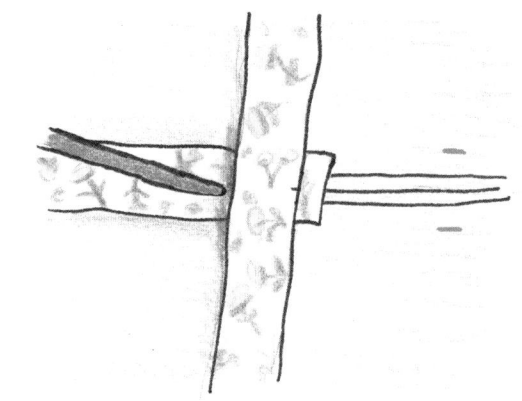

Fig 3

Adding the border

13 Measure the quilt top to check the size and adjust the border measurements if need be – see Adding a Border. From background fabric cut two pieces each 47in x 4in (119.4cm x 10.2cm) and machine sew them to the top and bottom of the quilt. Press the seams. From background fabric cut two pieces each 54in x 4in (137.2cm x 10.2cm) and machine sew them to each side of the quilt. Press the seams.

Appliquéing the border stems

14 Make stems on the bias – see Appliquéd Strips technique for details. Cut them into lengths of forty strips, with assorted fabrics 10in (25.4cm) long for the sides and eight strips of assorted fabrics each 15in (38.1cm) long for the corners.

15 The template pattern repeats five times on each side. The corner template is used on each corner. Along each side of the quilt one of the two intertwining stems has flowers and leaves appliquéd along it, to help disguise the seam between the border and the squares. To help in placing the sections of stem, use a fine interfacing such as Vilene, rather like tracing paper. Trace the corner template on to the interfacing, together with one segment of the intertwining stem in the corresponding position. Place over the quilt and pin at the top. Take a stem 10in (25.4cm) long and, using the interfacing as a placement guide, pin it in place. Join stems in the same way as the warps and wefts previously, making sure the joins are where the stems cross and are hidden beneath the other stem. Sew the stems on step by step – sewing one stem then the other, adding a new fabric strip as you go.

16 When appliquéing the border stems to the corners, take two 15in (38.1cm) strips and construct the knot and the strip passing through the knot. Use the interfacing as a guide. Make sure that the end of each stem tucks under the stems along the side. The corner strips are two complete pieces, with no joins at the actual knot. Sew the inside of the knot first, then the strip that passes through the knot, then the outside of the knot (see Fig 4A and 4B).

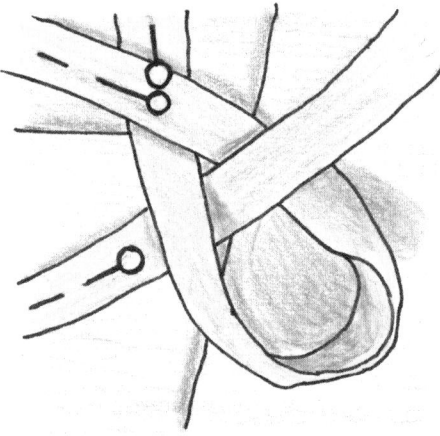

Fig 4A

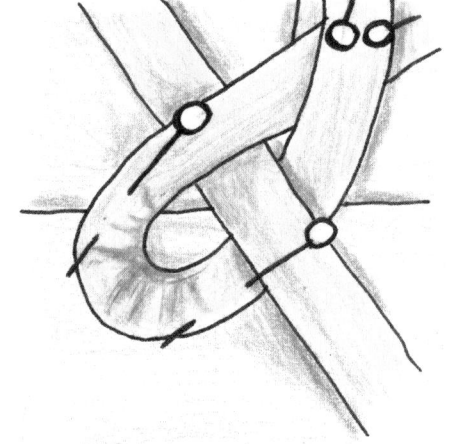

Fig 4B

Appliquéing the petals, flower bases and leaves

17 These shapes are made in the same way as the flowers on the squares, using the corner template. There are fifty-six flowers and forty-eight leaves in assorted yellows and greens. There is one flower and one leaf between each crossing of the stems, and the leaves alternately point towards and away from the quilt centre. Each flower has three petals and a flower base. At the corners there are four flowers. Appliqué two petals side by side and the third petal on top, with the pointed ends bunched up together. Sew the flower base over the top of the bases. Sew the flowers all facing the same way around the quilt. Sew the leaf on the same side of the stem as the flower. The dashed lines on the template show the pattern repeat.

Quilting and binding

18 Press the quilt and using the pieces of backing fabric and wadding (batting), follow the instructions in Making a Quilt Sandwich to fix the layers together.

19 Hand quilt in the ditch around all appliqué shapes and the woven strips, using a quilting thread that blends into the background – see Quilting. Quilt ¼in (6mm) out from the flowers in the centre of the squares in a green thread.

20 Finish your quilt with a binding as described in Binding. You will need to join five strips together, each 42in x 2½in (106.7cm x 6.3cm) long.

Buttercup Cushions

YOU WILL NEED

(For one cushion)

- Background fabric 42in x 24in (106.7cm x 61cm)
- Fabric for bias strip and flower bases 16in x 16in (40.6cm x 40.6cm)
- Fabric for appliqué leaves 10in x 10in (25.4cm x 25.4cm)
- Scraps of six different fabrics for petals (each flower needs about 4in/10.2cm square)
- Embroidery thread in colours to suit your fabrics
- Wadding (batting) 7½in x 7½in (19cm x 19cm)
- Circular cushion about 16in (40.6cm) diameter
- Basic kit

Finished size: 16in (40.6cm) in diameter approximately

Techniques used: appliqué using freezer paper, appliqué using templates, appliquéd strips, hand embroidery, hand quilting
Use ¼in (6mm) seams throughout

Templates: Buttercup Cushions

Preparing the background fabric and templates

1 Both cushions are made in the same way but in different designs (see templates). From background fabric, cut a rectangle 42in x 16in (106.7cm x 40.6cm), two 7½in (19cm) squares, and two strips 21in x 1½in (53.3cm x 3.8cm).

2 Enlarge the templates to full size. Trace the circle from the template on to freezer paper and the leaf, petal and petal base on to template plastic. Cut them out along the drawn line.

Making the cushion cylinder

3 Start with the fabric rectangle. Fold it in half, right sides together, so it is 21in x 16in (53.3cm x 40.6cm), making sure raw edges are aligned. Machine sew along the 16in (40.6cm) length to make a cylinder and press. At one end of the cylinder, make a hem for the drawstring to go through by folding in the raw edge by ¼in (6mm) and pressing. To make a neat gap for the drawstring, machine along the folded edge in one place for a distance of 1in (2.5cm). Fold in another ¾in (1.9cm) and press.

4 Pin and machine the hem just in from the edge, leaving a gap where the 1in (2.5cm) was sewn before. Set the sewing machine to a loose tension. Take the cylinder and, at the other end from the hem, machine two rows of stitches parallel to each other, sewing the first one ¼in (6mm) in from the raw edge and the second ½in (1.3cm) from the first. Sew both rows all the way round, leaving a good amount of spare thread at either end. Check at either end which threads are the pulling type and knot these in pairs. Evenly gather the fabric to a circle of 17in (43.2cm) circumference – see Fig 1. Knot the thread.

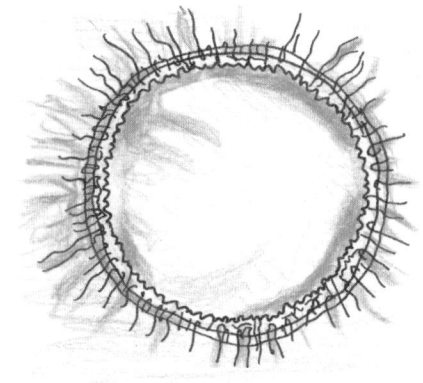

Fig 1

Adding the circle

5 Iron the freezer paper circle on to the wrong side of one of the 7½in (19cm) squares of background fabric. Place the two 7½in (19cm) squares of background fabric and the wadding (batting) on the table in this order: wadding, background piece (right side up) and background piece (freezer paper side up). Pin the three layers together. Carefully cut the circles out, cutting right up to the freezer paper. Remove the pins and freezer paper. Pin again then machine all the way round ¼in (6mm) in from the raw edge.

6 Carefully make little snips into the raw edge all the way round. Make a slit in the middle of one piece of background fabric and turn the circles inside out through it, easing the whole thing into a pleasing circle and press.

7 Pin and then machine the circle to cover the circular hole at the gathered end of the cylinder, using the gathered stitching as a guide. The side with the slit in it should be hidden on the inside, with the circle just covering the stitching (see Fig 2).

Appliquéing the stem

8 Make a ¼in (6mm) bias strip, 21in (53.3cm) long – see Appliquéd Strips. Hand appliqué the stem round the outside of the circle, covering the machine stitching. Make sure the two ends butt up against each other neatly. One of the flower bases will cover over this join later.

Preparing the petals

9 Cushion 1 and cushion 2 both have four flowers and each of these has three three-dimensional petals. Each cushion needs twenty-four petal shapes in total. Use your six fabrics, template plastic and the Appliqué using Templates technique, to make the petals.

Preparing the leaves and flower bases

10 Cushion 1 has four pairs of leaves, a flat one pointing into the circle and a three-dimensional one pointing outwards. For cushion 1 make twelve leaf shapes and four flower bases using template plastic. Make four three-dimensional leaves using eight of the leaf shapes, leaving four leaf shapes for the flat leaves. Cushion 2 has four pairs of three-dimensional leaves, along with the central circular strip. For cushion 2 make sixteen leaf shapes and four flower bases using template plastic. Make eight three-dimensional leaves using the leaf shapes.

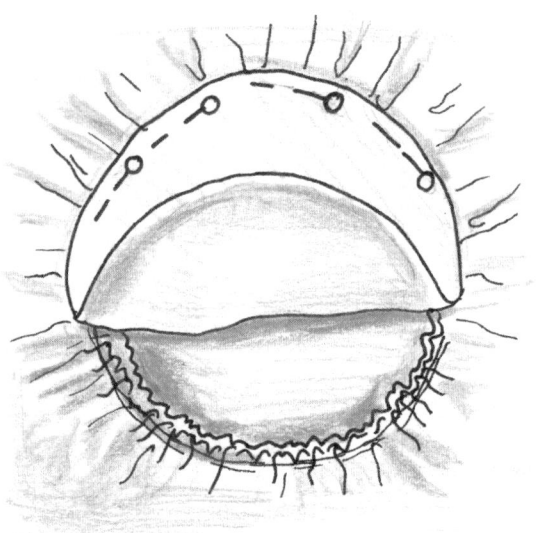

Fig 2

Appliquéing the petals, flower bases and leaves

11 For both cushion designs, take three of the petals of the same fabric and place them on top of the appliquéd circular strip where the join is. Hand sew the pointed end of the petals down, bunching them together as much as possible. Leave most of the petal free and standing up from the cushion cover. See photographs for positioning.

12 Cover the petal ends with a flower base. Sew right through all the layers in a number of places to anchor everything together. For cushion 1, appliqué a flat leaf a little below the flower base and facing in towards the centre of the circle. Sew a three-dimensional leaf opposite the flat leaf and facing away from the centre of the circle, so most of the leaf is free. Repeat for the other three flowers and leaf pairs, arranging them symmetrically around the circle. Embroider the veins on all the leaves, using vertical fly stitch (see Hand Embroidery). For cushion 2, position the leaves along the central circular strip, as shown in the template.

Making the drawstring

13 Cut out two pieces of background fabric each 21in x 1½in (53.3cm x 3.8cm) and join them to make a long strip. Press out the seam. Fold the fabric right sides together along the length of the strip making sure the edges are well aligned. Press the fold. Machine along one end and along the whole length ⅛in (3mm) in from the raw edge. Turn inside out, using something pointed to help you (I use a long piece of thin wooden dowel). Thread the drawstring through the opening of the hem.

Making the flower ends

14 Prepare six three-dimensional flower petals and four flower bases as before. Sew the petals to the end of the drawstring. Sew a flower base to either side of the drawstring. Open out the cushion cover cylinder and push the cushion into the bottom so that the appliqué is in the centre of the cushion. Pull up the drawstring and tie into a bow to finish.

Tools and Equipment

Basic tools and equipment are described here and a basic tool kit suggested. This can be added to as you discover other useful gadgets.

Basic Kit

You will need the following equipment for most of the projects in the book

- Pencil
- Erasable markers
- Fusible web
- Template plastic
- Freezer paper
- Tracing or greaseproof paper
- Quilting and embroidery threads
- Needles (hand and machine)
- Pins
- Thimble
- Scissors
- Rotary cutting equipment
- Fabric glue stick or spray glue
- Sewing machine
- Iron
- Light box (optional)

Measuring and cutting tools

For measuring and cutting out you will need a tape measure, a cutting mat, a rotary cutter, a long acrylic quilter's ruler and perhaps a square ruler too.

Marking tools

For marking up, use a water-soluble marker and a pencil. A crease marker, such as a hera, is also useful.

Sewing tools

You will need needles suitable for appliqué, embroidery and quilting, plus thin dressmaking pins and appliqué pins. A thimble will be needed, especially for hand quilting. You will need several pairs of scissors – one for cutting paper, one for fabric and embroidery scissors for snipping threads. An embroidery hoop, quilting hoop and quilting gloves are useful additions to the kit, though not essential.

Sewing machine

For most of the projects you will need a sewing machine, but there is no need for a high-tech one: the only stitches used are straight stitch, blanket stitch and blind hemming stitch. It has to have a darning foot for free-motion embroidery and quilting (you will also need to be able to lower the feed dogs), a walking foot for straight quilting and binding and an open appliqué foot for invisible appliqué and blanket stitch.

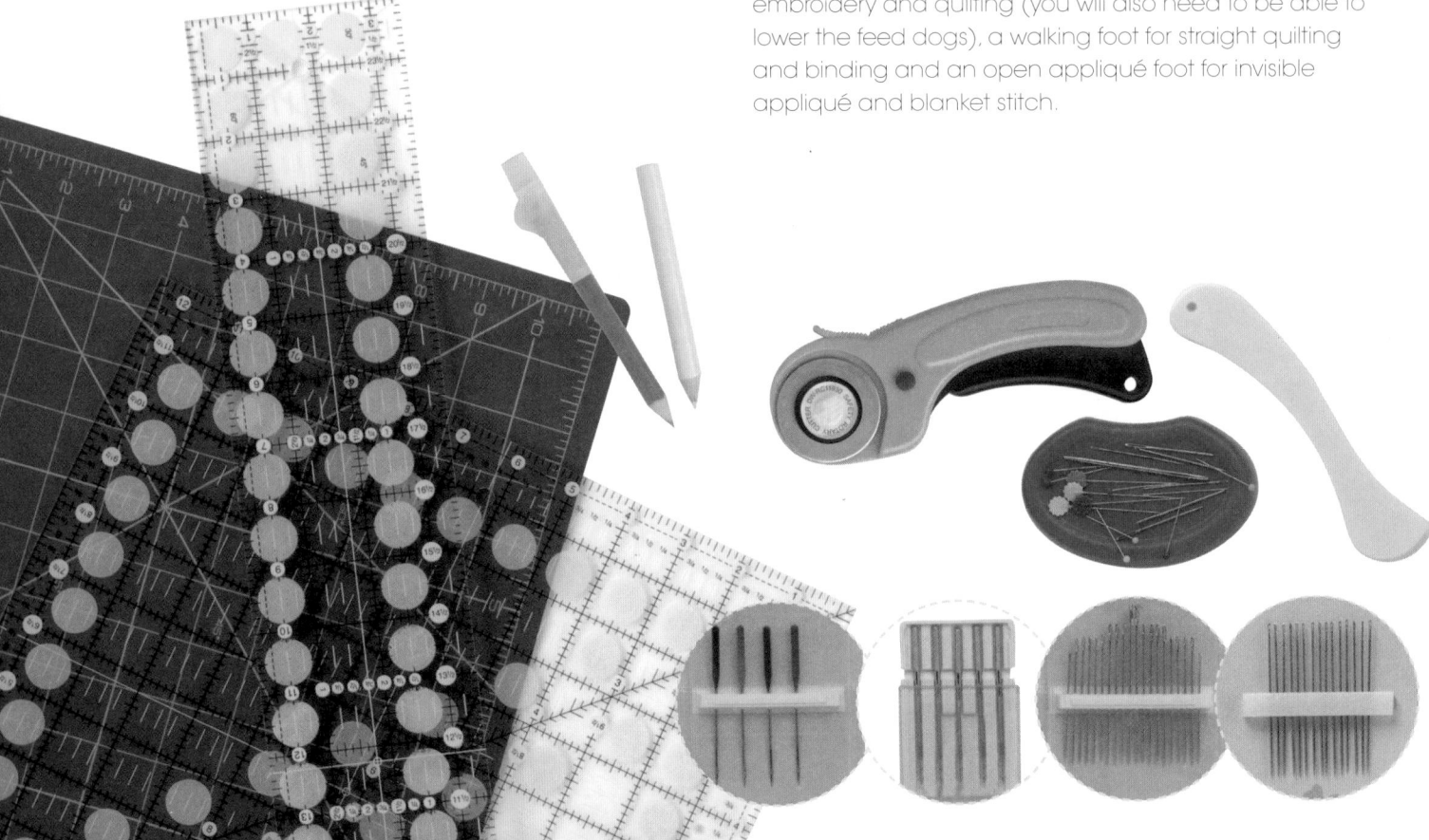

Threads

There are so many threads available for all sorts of patchwork, quilting and appliqué tasks. I've described here the threads I use but you may prefer other brands.

- For quilting: YLI hand quilting thread and YLI machine quilting thread.
- For invisible machine appliqué: YLI Wonder Invisible thread.
- For hand appliqué: YLI silk thread.
- For hand embroidery: DMC stranded cotton (floss) and silk ribbon in 2.5mm/3.5mm widths.
- For machine embroidery: Gütermann Sulky thread (cotton 30).

Fusible webs and stabilizers

Fusible web is used to fuse one fabric to another and is perfect for appliqué work. There are various brands available, such as Bondaweb. Stabilizers are products that can be fused or sewn to fabrics to create a firmer surface for stitching. I use the Stitch 'n' Tear brand.

Freezer paper

Freezer paper can be temporarily stuck to fabric by the heat of an iron and can be re-used several times. It has many uses and in this book I primarily use it as a template material, either on top of the fabric or underneath.

Tracing paper

This is useful for positioning various parts of an appliqué motif accurately. Trace the whole design on a master sheet and slip the appliqués under the paper in the positions they need to be sewn in. Greaseproof paper or a fine interfacing such as Vilene can be used in the same way.

Templates

Templates can be made of many materials and template plastic is very useful as the Mylar used can stand the heat of an iron. Some projects use metal washers in place of round templates.

Glues

A fabric glue stick and temporary adhesive spray (e.g. 505 brand) are useful for temporarily fixing appliqué motifs into place, and also for fixing the layers of a quilt sandwich together ready for quilting.

Needle felting tools

If you plan to do the felt project in the book and to decorate it with needle felting, you will need a special mat and tool. Needle felting is great fun and can be used for all sorts of decoration.

Light box

A light box is useful for tracing templates and designs but is not essential. You could use a brightly lit window instead.

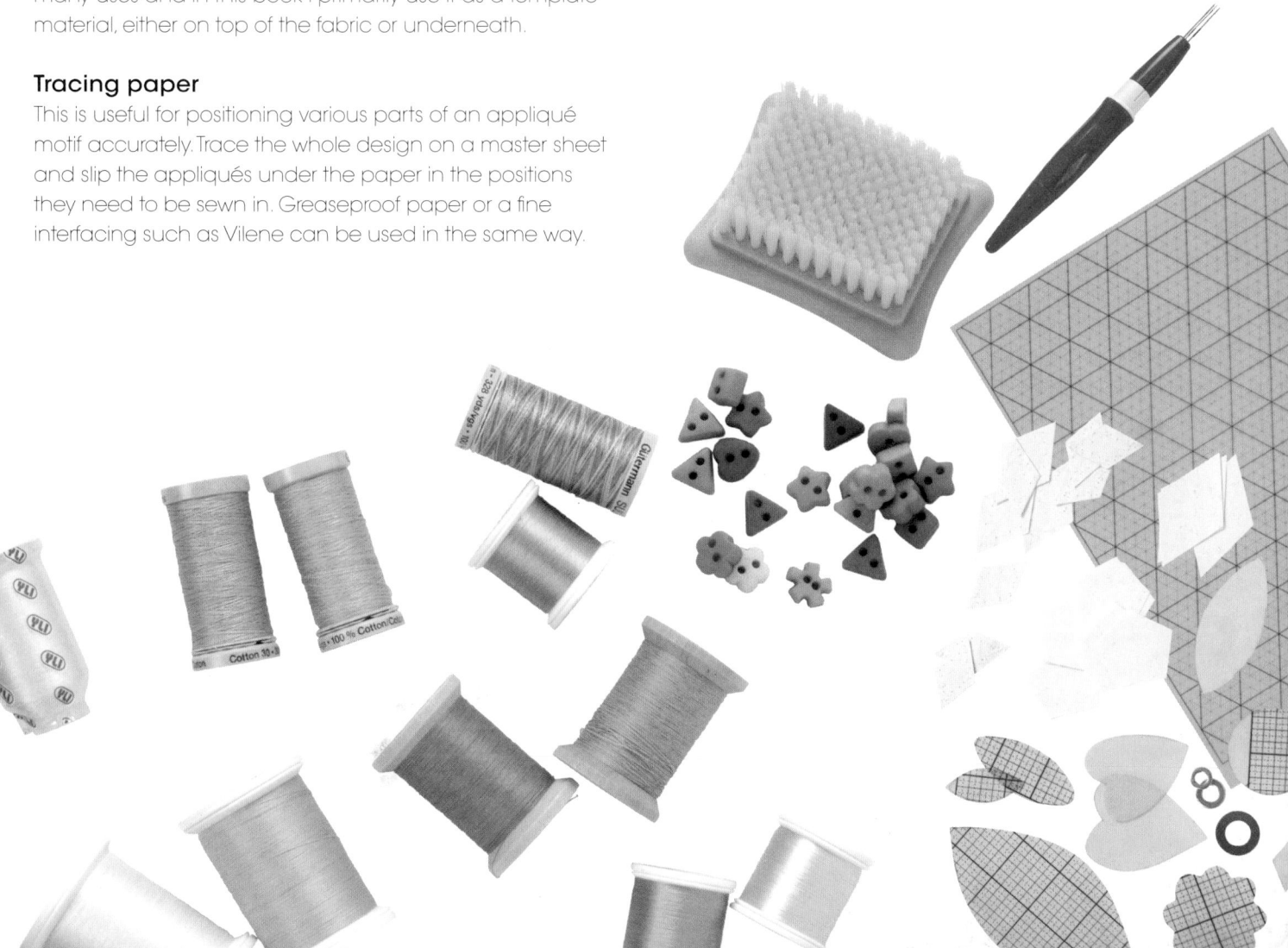

Techniques

This section describes the techniques you will need for the projects in this book, including simple piecing, embroidery and quilting, but with the emphasis on appliqué techniques.

Piecing Techniques

The projects use various easy piecing techniques. If a technique is only used once for a single project it is described in the relevant chapter.

Simple Machine Piecing

Piecing is the joining together of pieces of fabric, whether they are squares, rectangles, triangles or a combination of many shapes. Cut the shapes as accurately as possible and machine sew together with a ¼in (6mm) seam allowance. Where seams meet make sure they are pressed in opposite directions for a smooth finish and in order that units or blocks fit together better – see diagram below.

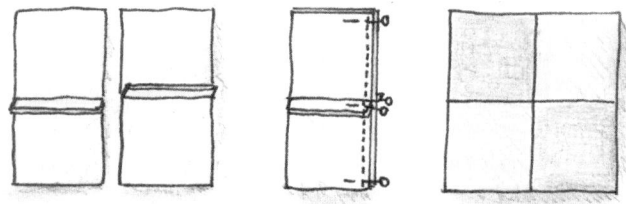

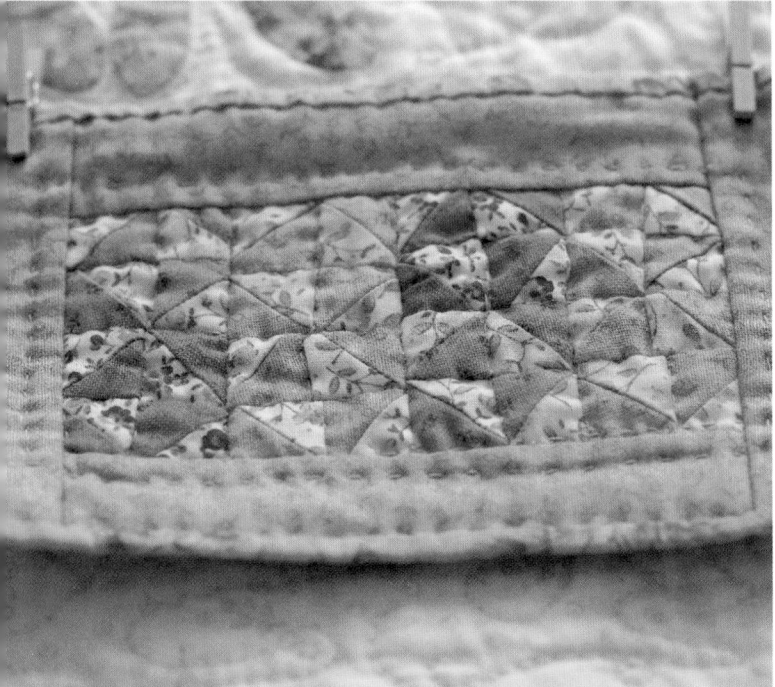

English Paper Piecing

English paper piecing is a method of piecing together a number of the same shape where accuracy is required, for instance where six diamonds are joined to make a star, or where hexagons are joined together in a honeycomb pattern. Thick paper templates are used which can be bought in packets or be made at home. Magazine covers are good for this.

1 Place the template on the back of the fabric and draw accurately round the shape. Remove the template and cut out the fabric ¼in (6mm) out from the drawn line.

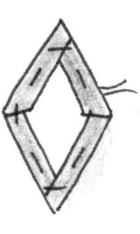

Fig 1

2 Place the template back within the drawn marks. Bring the excess fabric over the edges of the template so it is smooth and taut all the way round the shape. Tack (baste) all round through all layers.

3 Join two pieces by placing them right sides together, with the edges to be joined lined up and then over sew with small stitches that will not show when you open the pieces. Open them out, and join another piece by placing it right sides together with one of the existing pieces, lining up the edge to be joined. Over sew in the same way. Continue until all the pieces required are joined. Don't remove the papers until the end. The order in which the edges should be joined depends on the design. For a diamond star it's a good idea to make two sets of three diamonds first and then join the two halves together.

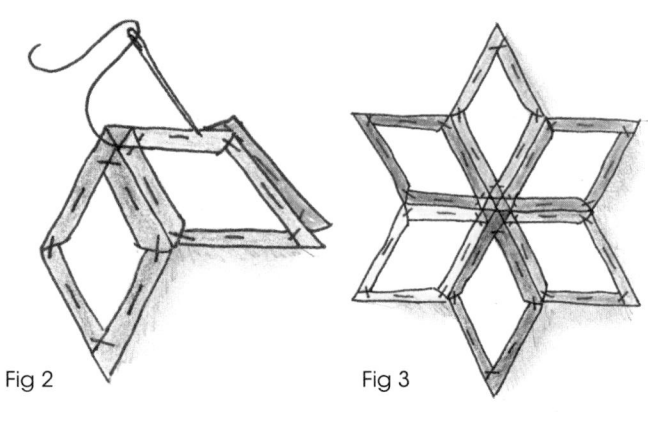

Fig 2   Fig 3

Foundation Piecing Triangle Strips

This technique involves sewing directly on to a marked paper foundation, which helps to make a strip of triangles come out straight and true. Ordinary paper can be used but a product called Stitch 'n' Tear is easier. A light box is useful to see the lines on the paper. Where foundation piecing is used in the projects, a template is provided for cutting out the triangles, and also a template for the paper foundation for a strip of triangles.

1 Using the triangle template make a template from template plastic. Note that the template shows the cutting line, not the sewing line. Use it to mark out triangles, making sure that the longest side of the triangle is along the grain of the fabric or at right angles to it. Place the triangles on a work top in the order required.

2 To join the triangles into strips, take the template for the strips and trace it on to the paper. The diagonal lines on the template are sewing lines. Each time a triangle is added make sure that it overlaps its diagonal line by ¼in (6mm). The edges of the template are cutting lines for trimming the strip at the end, and the dotted lines indicate where the finished strips will be sewn to the panels. Cut out the paper strip close to the outline.

3 Now the triangles have to be systematically sewn on to the foundation, as follows. Place the first triangle on to the back of the paper (the blank side) so it overlaps where the first line is on the other side of the paper, as shown in Fig 1. Place the second triangle face down on top of the first and at right angles (Fig 2). Now turn the whole thing over and sew along the first line, joining the triangles to the paper and to each other (Fig 3). Note: to the right of the sewing line there should be a ¼in (6mm) seam.

4 Turn the whole thing over again, fold down the second triangle and place a third triangle face down on top, as in Fig 4, so there is ¼in (6mm) extra fabric to the right of the diagonal line on the paper. Trim back the excess fabric from the triangles that have been sewn on before.

5 Turn it back to the wrong side and machine along the next line. Continue with the next triangle and so on until there is the required number. Trim the completed strip to the cutting line on the template. Remove the paper and press the work.

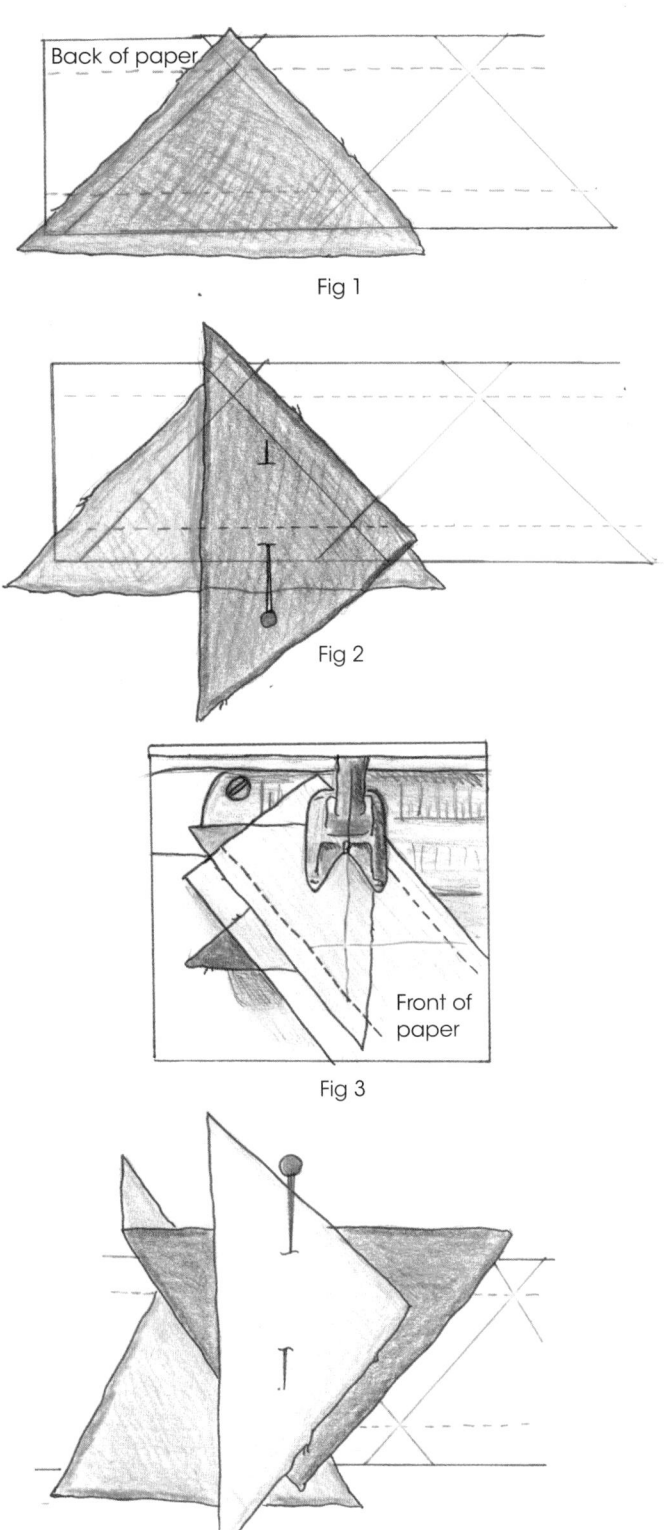

Back of paper

Fig 1

Fig 2

Front of paper

Fig 3

Fig 4

Adding a Border

You often need to surround a quilt panel with a border of fabric. The width of the border is sometimes not crucial, so if there is any inaccuracy in the size of the panel, there is an opportunity to correct this by adjusting the size of the border. For this reason it is wise not to cut out the border pieces until the panel is ready. Narrow borders around blocks are called sashing and can be sewn on in the same way as a border.

1 Measure the height of the panel or quilt top you are going to surround by the border, raw edge to raw edge. Measure at several different points and take a rough average. Cut two strips of border fabric as long as the width of the panel, and as wide as the border is to be when finished, plus a seam allowance. If the border is to be at the outside of the completed quilt, then the seam allowance is ¼in (6mm). If there is to be another border around it, the seam allowance is ½in (1.3cm). Join these strips to the top and bottom of the panel (Fig 1).

Fig 1

2 Now measure the quilt from top to bottom, including the borders just added, raw edge to raw edge. Cut two more strips of border fabric to this measurement and the same width as the other strips. Join these to the sides of the quilt (Fig 2).

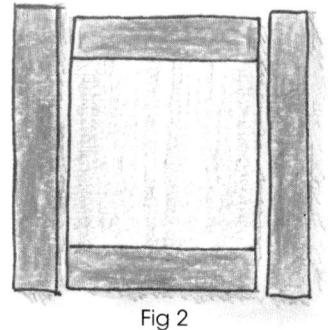

Fig 2

Appliqué Techniques

There are many appliqué techniques, some hand and some machine, and they differ in how difficult or quick they are. This section describes those used for the projects in this book.

Positioning Appliqué Pieces

When placing appliqué pieces on your background fabric you can place them by eye or trace the complete template on to fine Vilene or a product called Pattern Ease and place this tracing on top of your background fabric to get the positioning right. In the case of fusible web you can use greaseproof paper for this purpose.

Sometimes an appliqué template will be made up of several pieces. You don't need to cut it out as it looks but use simple, more rounded shapes, and fuse or sew them on in overlapping layers.

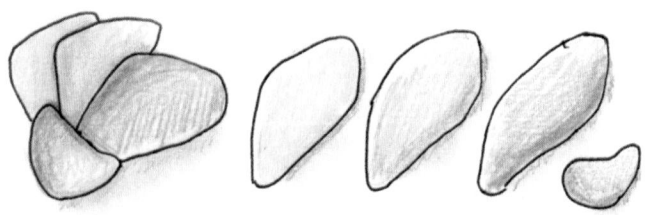

Fig 1

Appliqué using Fusible Web

Fusible web is a type of paper with thin glue on one side, which melts with the heat of an iron to fuse one fabric piece to another, and so can be used to attach appliqué. There are various brands, one of which is Bondaweb (also called Wonder Under and Vliesofix). The shape you want to make is drawn on the papery side and ironed on to the appliqué fabric. The shape is then cut out, the paper peeled off, and the glue side ironed on to the background fabric. Appliqué pieces can be finished off by sewing around the edge by hand or machine.

Fusible web produces a flat effect and is quite quick. The edge is left raw, so no hemming is required. This also means you use less material than for other appliqué techniques, so if using another technique where a seam allowance is required you will need to allow for this when calculating the amounts of material needed for a pattern. Use fusible web as follows.

1 Trace the shape or shapes needed on to the back of the template, using a light box or window. (This step isn't necessary if pieces are symmetrical as you can work from the front of the template.)

2 Place the fusible web over the shape on the back of the template (or sometimes the front, see above) and trace the shape or shapes on to the papery side. If there is just one shape of a particular fabric, roughly cut out the web with extra space all around. If there are a number of shapes that will use the same fabric, group them together on a single piece of web, making sure that they are not drawn right up to the edge.

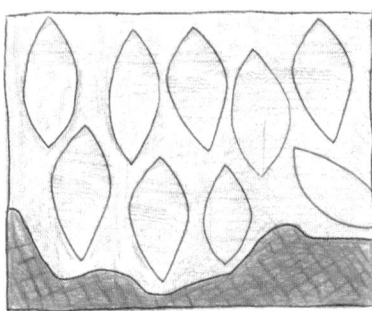

Fig 1

3 Place the fusible web on to the back of the chosen fabric, rough side down, and iron in place. It's a good idea to put greaseproof paper down on to the ironing board first to protect the board and iron.

4 Cut out the shape along the drawn line, so there is a fabric piece with web attached. Peel off the papery side and carefully place the piece on the background. Do this by eye in simple cases, but for a more complicated pattern it's a good idea to trace on to greaseproof paper the template for the whole picture (or a large part of it) and pin this in place to the background by its edges. The individual pieces with their web can then be carefully slipped under the greaseproof paper template and placed accurately before ironing on.

Fig 2

5 Iron on to your background fabric using a hot, dry iron. If you make a mistake you may be able to remove it if you're quick, but once ironed on and cool it will be firmly stuck. Take care, as newly ironed pieces are *very* hot.

6 Sew round the shape using blanket stitch on the machine or by hand. It helps when blanket stitching on the machine round small pieces to go slowly and to wear quilting gloves to give greater control. Start with the needle in the fabric and bring up the bobbin thread, then put the thread out of your way. I use an open-toe appliqué foot on the machine.

Appliqué using Freezer Paper

Freezer paper is a stiff, shiny paper that was originally designed to wrap food in, but is now widely used for appliqué. It is typically used for hand appliqué but can also be used with invisible machine appliqué, as described in the next section. It can be used either *underneath* the appliqué piece or *on top* of the piece.

Freezer paper underneath

1 For this method, trace the shape or shapes needed on to the back of the template, using a light box or window. (This step isn't strictly necessary if the pieces concerned are symmetrical – in this case you can work from the front of the template.)

2 Place the freezer paper shiny side down over the back (or sometimes the front, see above) of the template and trace around the shape to be appliquéd.

3 Cut the shape out of the paper (no seam allowance at this stage). Place the fabric right side down, and place the paper shape shiny side *down* on to the fabric. Iron the paper on to the fabric using a dry iron. The shiny side of the paper will stick temporarily to the fabric. Repeat for several shapes if you wish, being sure to allow ¼in (6mm) all around each shape for seams.

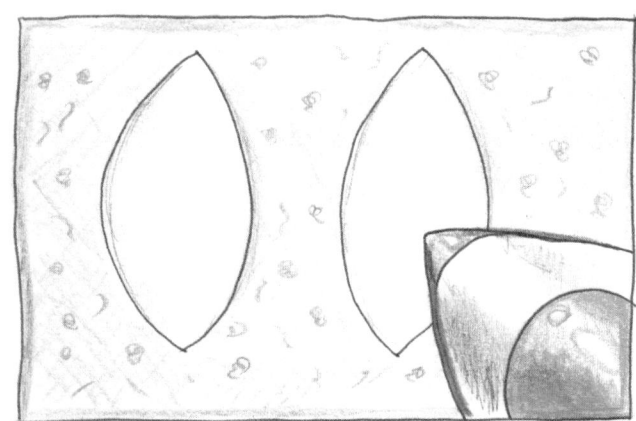

Fig 1

4 Cut out the fabric shape, adding ¼in (6mm) all round for seams. Fold the raw edge of the piece over the paper and tack (baste) the edge down all the way around through the three layers and press well. The shape is now ready to be sewn to the background fabric.

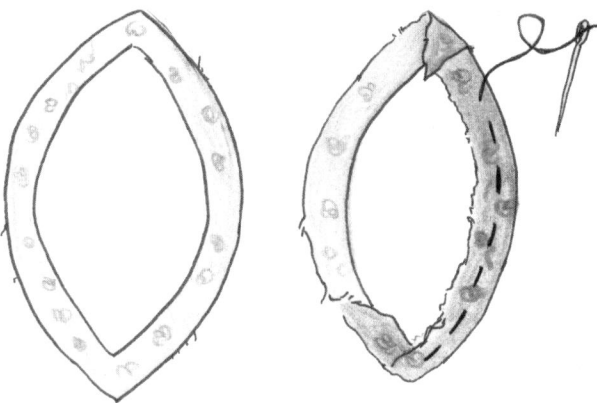

Fig 2

5 If you are sewing by hand, in order to get an invisible stitch, take your needle up through the main fabric, through the shape and back down into the main fabric at the same place that it came out. Sew halfway around the shape, remove tacking and paper, and then carry on sewing around the shape.

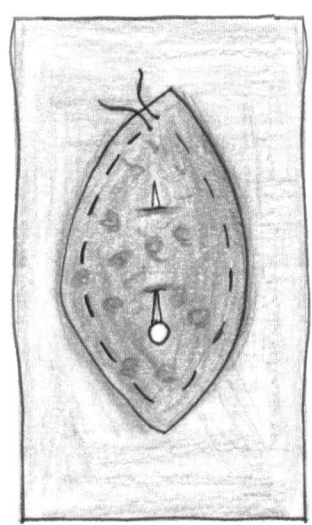

Fig 3

Freezer paper on top

This is simpler than the previous method but not quite as accurate and not as suitable for complicated shapes. The freezer paper has to be stuck down really well for it to work.

1 Place the freezer paper shiny side *down* over the front of the template. Trace around the shape to be appliquéd using a light box or window. Cut the shape out of the paper (with no seam allowance at this stage). Place the fabric right side up, and place the paper shape shiny side *down* on to the fabric. Iron the paper on to the fabric using a dry iron. The shiny side of the paper will stick temporarily to the fabric. Repeat for several shapes if you wish, being sure to allow ¼in (6mm) all round each shape for seams. Cut out the fabric shape, adding ¼in (6mm) all round for seams. Fold the raw edge of the piece under and tack (baste) in place, leaving the paper on top and press well.

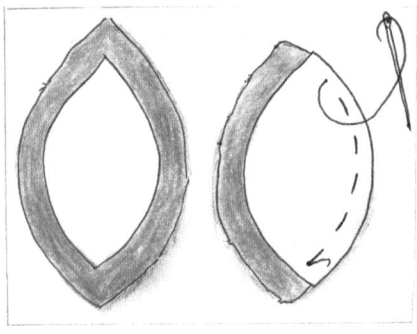

Fig 1

2 The shape can now be sewn to the background. If sewing by hand, in order to get an invisible stitch, take your needle up through the main fabric, through the shape, and back down into the main fabric at the same place that it came out. Remove the paper and tacking (basting). Alternatively iron the paper on the front of the fabric, cut out with ¼in (6mm) seam allowance. Tack all round the shape halfway between the edge of the paper and the raw edge. Pull the tacking tight to make the leaf shape. Remove the paper before sewing.

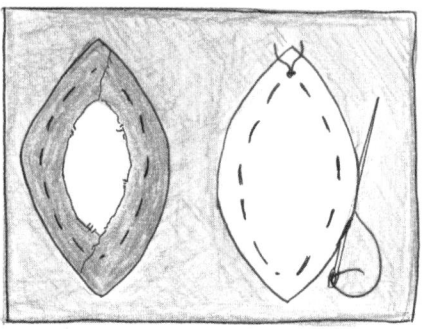

Fig 2

Appliqué using Templates

An alternative to the freezer paper technique is to use a template cut from template plastic or, for a round piece, use a washer or a coin. This technique gives as neat results as the freezer paper underneath method, and is very convenient when you are making many identical pieces.

1 If you are making a piece that isn't round, place the template plastic over the front of the template and trace around the shape you are to appliqué, using a light box or window. Cut the shape out of the plastic (with no seam allowance at this stage). In the case of leaves, blunt the ends slightly to stop the points poking through the fabric.

2 Place the fabric right side down and place the plastic shape (or coin or washer) on to the fabric. In the case of shapes that are not symmetrical, make sure you put the plastic template the right way up so the finished piece will be the right way round. Draw around the plastic shape (or coin or washer). Repeat if you wish for several shapes, leaving room for ¼in (6mm) all round each piece.

3 Cut out the fabric shape, adding ¼in (6mm) all round for seams. If the shape curves inwards, for instance at the top of a heart shape, cut a little snip into the seam allowance at the concave part (as shown in the diagram below), and make sure you start the tacking near that place. Tack all around the piece halfway between the edge of the piece and the drawn edge of the finished shape.

4 Place the plastic shape (or coin or washer) back in place, fold the edges of the piece over it and pull the tacking (basting) tight so that the shape is trapped inside. If you are using a coin, washer or Mylar template plastic, you can press the piece with an iron (use a number 1 setting for Mylar). If you are using ordinary template plastic you can simply finger press it.

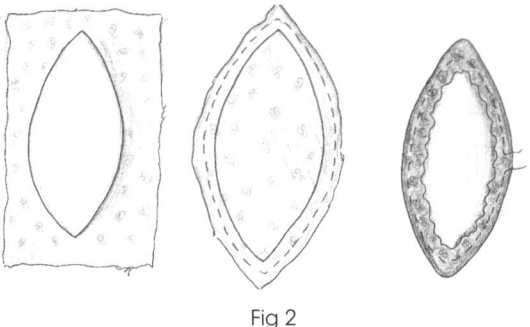

Fig 2

5 Loosen the tacking enough to take out the template, then re-tighten and knot the thread, leaving the piece with its seam neatly tucked under, and press well. The shape is now ready to be sewn to the background. If sewing by hand, in order to get an invisible stitch, take your needle up through the main fabric, through the shape and back down into the main fabric at the same place it came out.

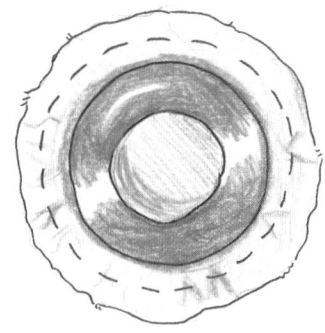

Fig 3

Fig 1

Machine Appliqué using Invisible Thread

This technique uses the sewing machine to attach a piece you have prepared in the same way as for hand appliqué. It depends on your machine being able to do a blind hemming stitch and having an open-toe appliqué foot. With care it can be made to look almost like hand appliqué and is much quicker. For the top bobbin of the machine use nylon invisible thread, such as YLI Wonder Invisible thread (I use neutral). For the bottom bobbin use a normal thread the colour of the background fabric. When you get to a corner, if you think you are going to overrun you can lift your foot off the pedal and ease the stitch using the hand wheel. You could also experiment with a zigzag stitch instead of a straight one.

1 Prepare the piece using one of the freezer paper or template methods described before. If using freezer paper, remove it from the piece before sewing down. Fix in place temporarily with a glue stick or tack (baste) it in place.

2 Carefully machine around the shape using invisible thread and blind hemming stitch and an open-toe appliqué foot (*not* a blind hemming foot), making sure that the stitching runs exactly along the edge of the piece. Remove the tacking if applicable.

Hand Appliqué using Needle-Turn

This freehand technique takes some practise to perfect, but it is less complicated than other techniques and is particularly suited to very small pieces.

1 Draw the shape you want to make directly on to the fabric. You can choose either to mark the front or the back of the fabric – being careful to get shapes the right way round. If you mark the front. Use a marker that can be removed, such as a water-soluble marker. You could trace directly from a template using a light box or window, or if making many copies of the same shape it may be worth making a plastic template and drawing around that. Cut out the shape, allowing only 1/8in (3mm) for the seam.

2 Sew the appliqué directly on to the background, tucking the seam under as you go by poking it under with the needle. If you marked the front of the fabric you can use the line as a guide when sewing. If you marked the back (which avoids having to remove the mark later) you will depend on your ability to judge the size of the seam as you go.

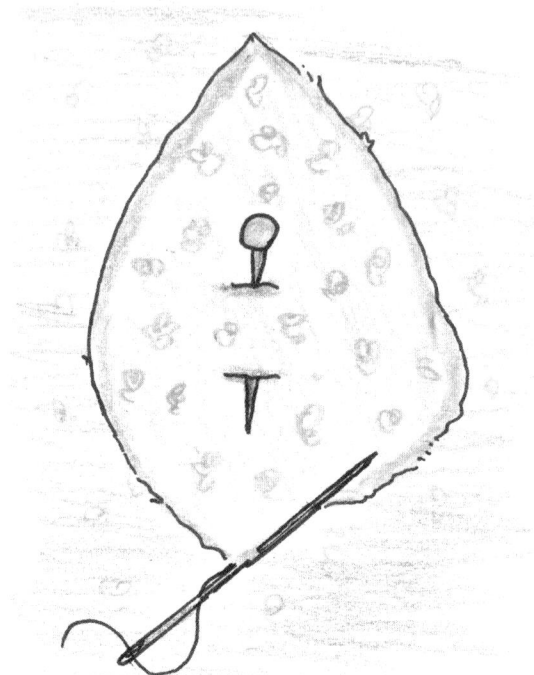

Appliquéd Strips

Many of my designs use narrow appliqué strips for flower stems, fence posts and so on, some curved and some straight. Since they are narrow, the normal appliqué techniques don't work as well. In the case of curved strips such as stems, rather than cutting a curved strip it is more convenient to cut a straight strip diagonally across the fabric, that is, on the bias, which has more stretch in it. This strip can then be curved as you sew it on. With a fusible web, cut a strip the width required, with no seam allowance. Otherwise follow these instructions, which are for ¼in (6mm) stems. Note: if you want ⅛in (3mm) stems, move the ruler along ⅛in (3mm) rather than ¼in (6mm), and similarly adjust the measurements for ½in (1.3cm) strips.

1 Make sure the fabric has a straight edge to work from. If you are cutting on the bias this will mean making an initial cut at 45 degrees diagonally across the fabric. For straight strips cut either straight along the grain of the fabric or at right angles across it.

2 Line up a ruler and the fabric lengthways so the ruler edge is ¼in (6mm) in from the fabric edge. Using a hera marker or other firm-edged implement, score along the ruler to produce a good crease (Fig 1).

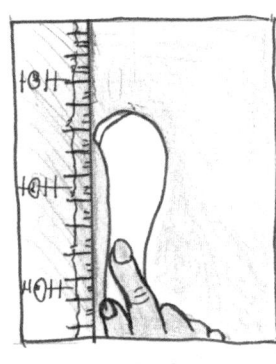

Fig 1

3 Move the ruler ¼in (6mm) from the crease line just drawn and score again (Fig 2).

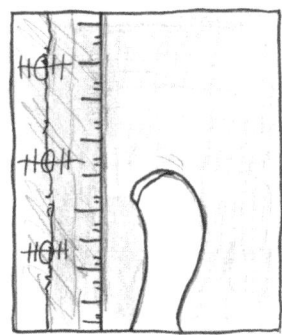

Fig 2

4 Move the ruler again ¼in (6mm) from the crease line, and this time cut with a rotary cutter (Fig 3). Repeat the process to produce as many strips as needed. Now fold each strip into three lengthways, following the creases, and press well. Sew the strips to the background either by hand or machine.

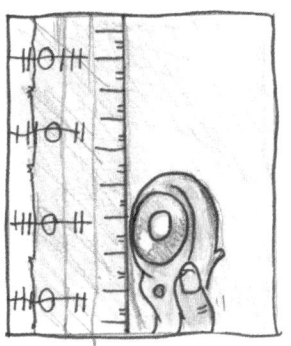

Fig 3   Fig 4

This pretty cushion uses an appliquéd strips technique (see the Woven Baskets chapter) and the same templates. Shadow quilting in a thread to match the background radiates out from the basket. The cover is bound with a print fabric to match one of the strips in the basket.

Embroidery Techniques

Generally, embroidery is done on the quilt top before it is tacked (basted) and quilted, but sometimes, if you want a 'puffy' effect, you can embroider through the top and the wadding, before both are tacked to the backing fabric. If you sew through all three layers of course, it counts as quilting, and you can get similar effects with that.

Machine Embroidery

Machine embroidery can be as complicated as you like with a modern machine, but in this book I've only used simple freehand embroidery using a darning foot with the feed dogs disengaged. This technique is ideal for when appliqué pieces have been bonded on with fusible web and sewn down.

Use a heavier needle and if possible quilting gloves so your hands don't slip. Generally, a stabilizer is needed on the back of the background fabric to stop it puckering up. Plan designs so that as much as possible they can be embroidered in a single continuous line, as this reduces the chore of sewing in ends later. This will probably mean you use loops a lot and go over the same line several times. It is best to work out the general pattern on paper first and practise on spare fabric, prepared to be like the stabilized/bonded fabric that will be worked on for real.

Choose thread that is subtle and doesn't dominate too much. To stop the bobbin thread tangling with your stitches, place the fabric under the darning foot and lower it. Turning the machine slowly by hand, bring the thread up through the fabric and move it out of the way. Now place your gloved hands quite close to the darning foot and draw the design gently over the area in a flowing manner. It is a balancing act between pedal control and hand movement. If the pattern changes slightly and does its own thing don't worry. When stopping, allow extra thread for sewing in. Take the thread through to the back and then knot right up to the fabric.

Hand Embroidery

I find using an embroidery hoop really helpful for hand embroidery as I have more control over what is going on, with a certain amount of tension as I am making the stitches. It also helps to keep the wadding (batting) in place, if I'm embroidering through the wadding. I use two strands of DMC stranded cotton (floss) for hand stitches. The projects in this book use only very simple hand embroidery, with the following stitches: back stitch, blanket stitch, lazy daisy stitch, French knots, fly stitch, stem stitch, straight stitch and satin stitch. These are illustrated here.

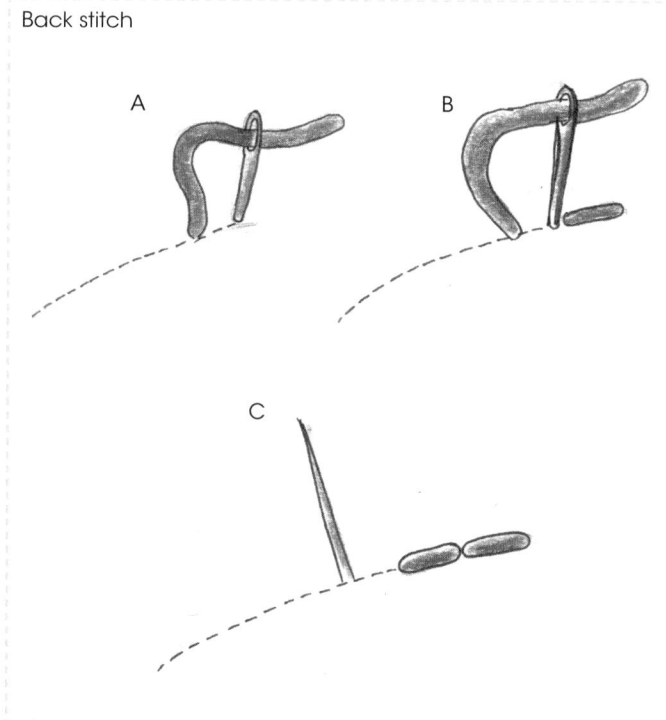

Back stitch

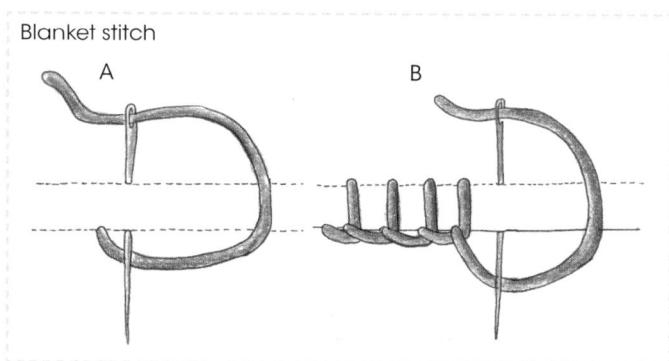

Blanket stitch

Lazy daisy stitch

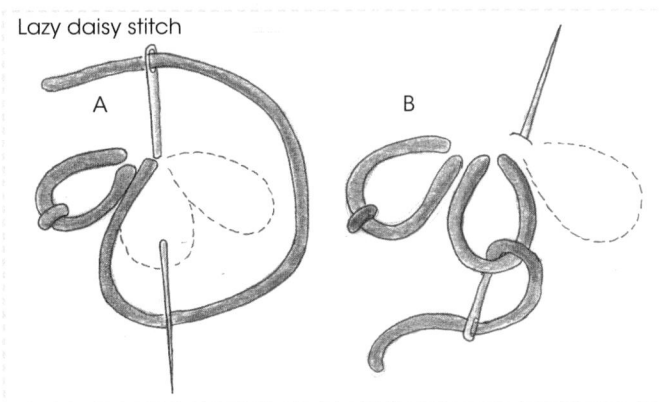

Satin stitch

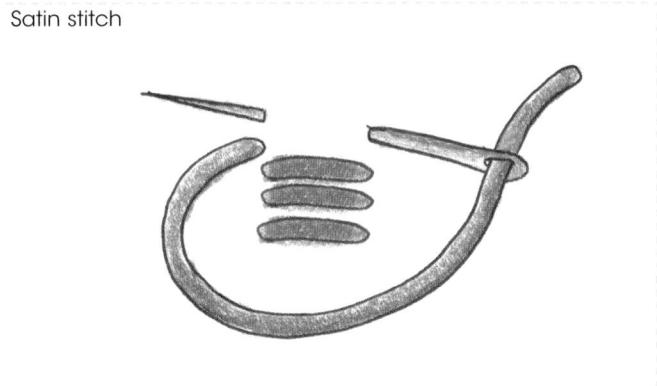

Fly stitch (vertical)

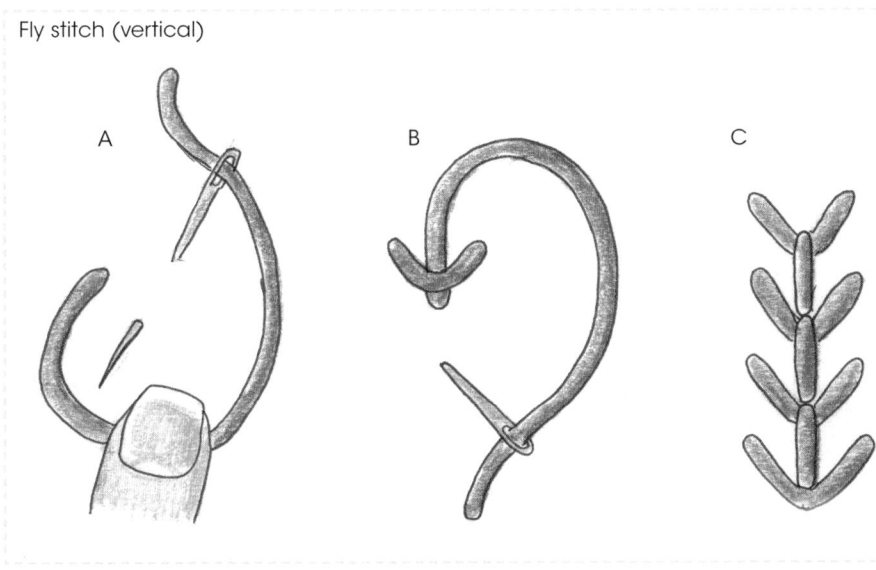

Stem stitch

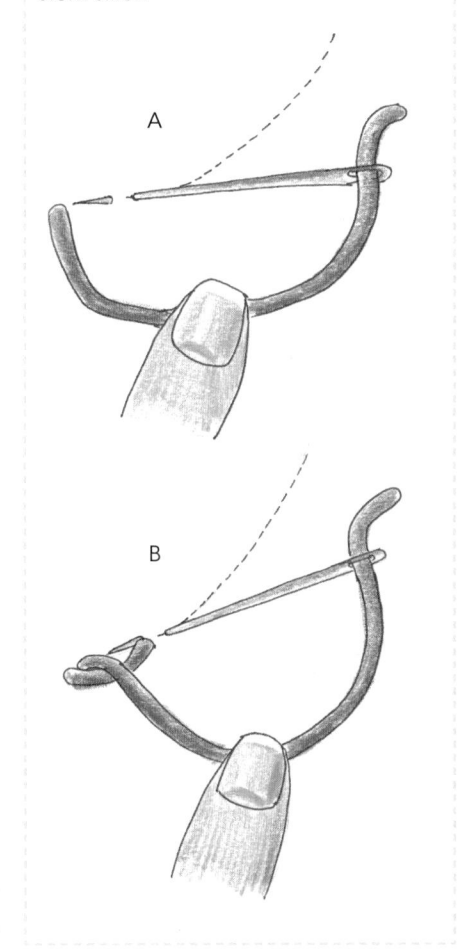

French knots

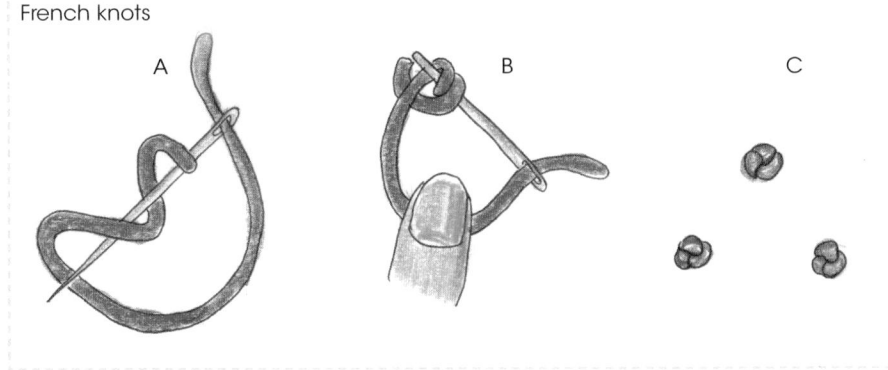

Seed stitch

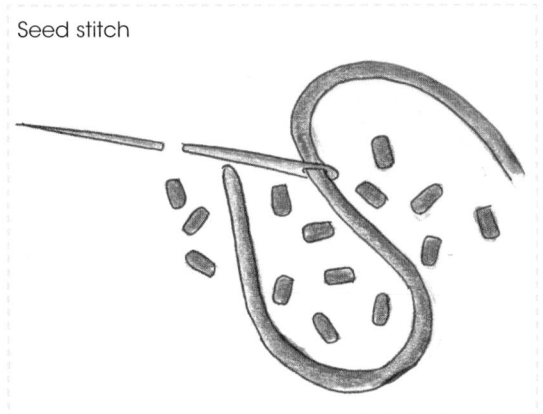

Straight stitch

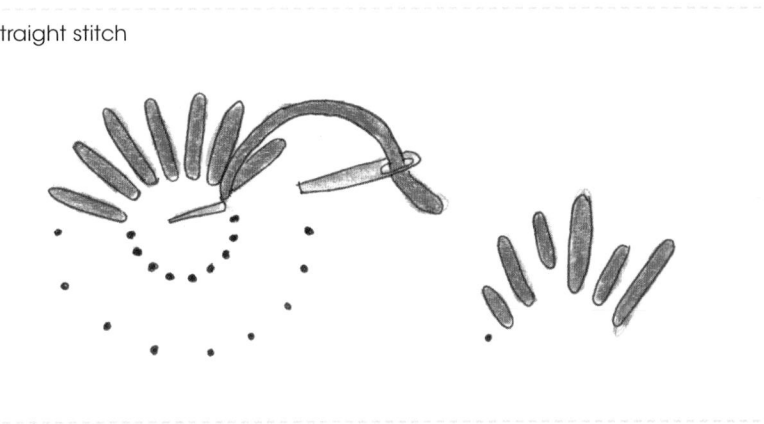

Needle Felting

The technique described here is for decorating felt by tangling wool tops into it. It is used in the Feathered Friends Quilt, for decorating the birds' breasts. You will need a needle felting mat, a pen-style needle felting tool and small amounts of wool tops. Various yarns and fibres can be used for felting so ask at your local craft shop. Generally a stabilizer is needed at the back of the work, but in the case of the bird quilt there was no need as the felt was fused to the brushed cotton and appliquéd in place.

1 Put the felting mat on a flat surface. Place the part of the bird that is to be felted on top of the mat. Make sure the area to be felted is in the centre of the mat, not at the edge.

2 Take a small amount of wool tops about the size of a little fingernail and mould the fibre into a flattish circle. Place on the bird or motif where you want the circle to be. Take the needle felting tool, remove the paper between the needles and stab the wool into the felt of the bird with an upright movement (see diagram below). It's important that the stabbing motion isn't too fierce as the needles are very sharp. Keep doing this, manipulating the fibres to keep it a circle. Tufts of the stabbed fibres will be seen on the back of the work.

3 Once all the felting that is needed has been done, machine embroider the area carefully with a delicate pattern, over the felted area to keep it all in place.

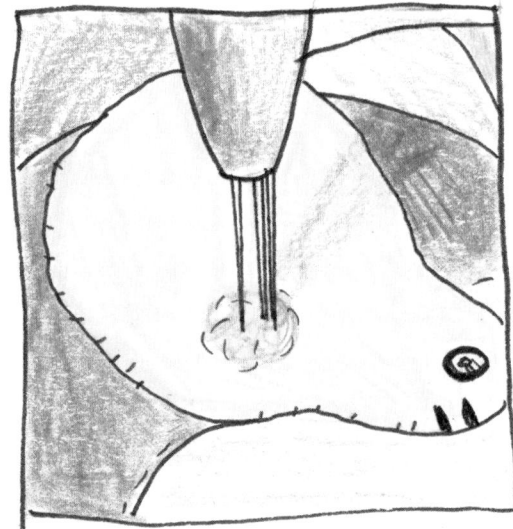

Quilting Techniques

There are various ways to quilt and we all have our favourites. For the projects in this book I used hand and machine techniques, including quilting in the ditch, crosshatch quilting, shadow quilting and freehand free-motion quilting. Preparing the layers of the quilt well beforehand is an important part of the process.

Making a Quilt Sandwich

A quilt sandwich is a term used to describe the joining together of the quilt top, the wadding (batting) and the backing, holding them in place temporarily.

Cut out the backing and the wadding (batting) a little larger than the quilt top, about 2in (5.1cm) all round, and sandwich the three together, right sides outwards. Smooth them together to get rid of wrinkles and join the layers either by large tacking (basting) stitches all over the quilt in a grid pattern (see diagram below), or with safety pins or with plastic tags made for the purpose.

Alternatively, especially for a small quilt, you can use spray glue. In this case, pin or clamp the backing fabric, right side down, on to a flat surface and spray all over with the glue spray. Add the wadding, gradually easing it down, working out from the middle or from one side to the other to avoid wrinkles. Spray the wadding with the glue and carefully add the quilt top in a similar way.

Quilting

Quilting is the method by which the three layers of a quilt are joined together permanently by sewing through the layers, covering most or all of the quilt with stitches. You can quilt by hand or by machine. For my taste hand quilting gives a beautiful result. It takes longer than machining but it's worth it if you're making something special.

For hand quilting use a simple running stitch, similar to tacking only with smaller stitches. A quilting frame is helpful but not essential.

For machine quilting, some modern machines will quilt in complicated patterns, but if, like me, you have a more basic machine use a simple stitch with a walking foot if quilting in straight lines, or a darning foot if you want to make curves or create free-motion patterns. As far as possible when machine quilting, make the quilting one continuous line of stitching, as this reduces the need to sew in ends. This may sometimes mean retracing your steps. Quilters' gloves are useful, giving you more control.

Crosshatched quilting

This is a pattern where the quilting is in straight lines at right angles, either vertically and horizontally or diagonally.

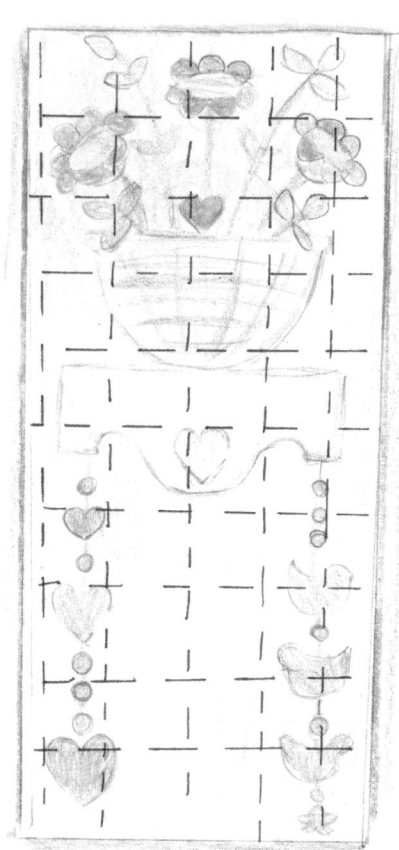

Freehand quilting

The design might be a pattern that roughly repeats, as shown in the first picture below. You can quilt in the form of a picture. In this case you may wish to mark the quilting pattern first. Use a marker that will come out in water or that will rub out.

Shadow quilting

This is the technique where a line of stitches is quilted all around a piece of appliqué, perhaps ⅛in to ¼in (3mm to 6mm) from its edge. Another line is then quilted all around this line, the same distance out, repeating the process until the quilting meets the edge of the quilt, or perhaps the shadow quilting surrounding another appliqué piece. It is also called echo quilting.

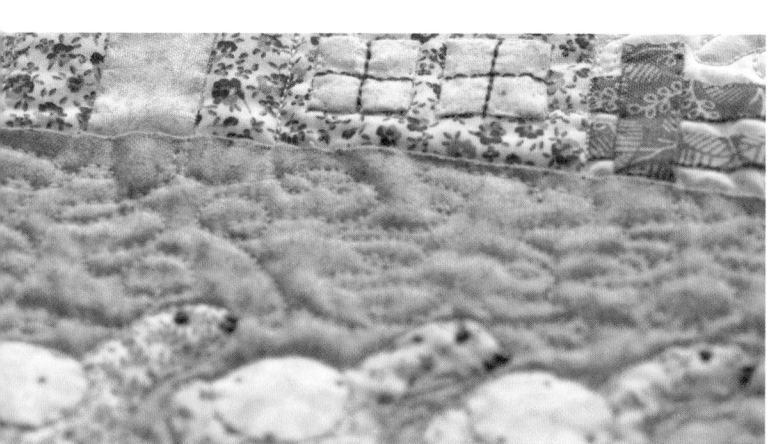

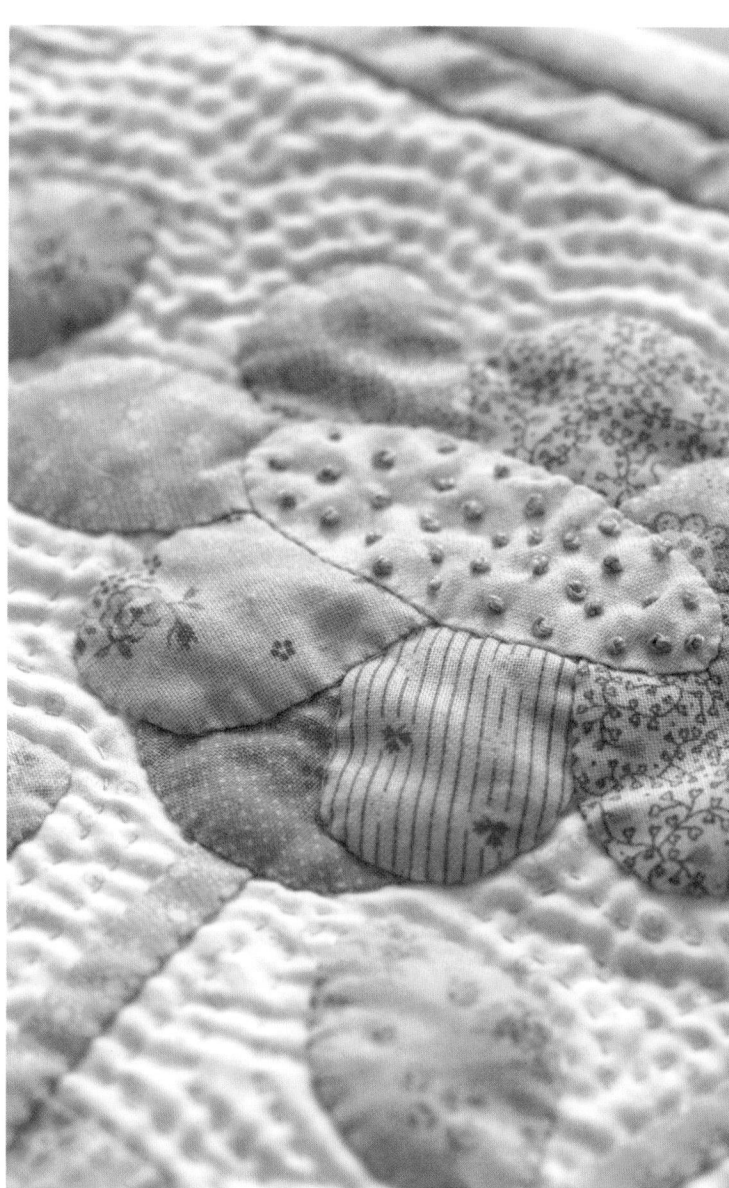

Quilting in the ditch

This is a technique where the quilting itself is invisible because you stitch right on top of the stitches which attach the appliqué piece to the background fabric, or in the seams of a pieced quilt. This has the effect of making the appliqué piece 'puff up' slightly, giving a lovely three-dimensional effect.

Finishing Techniques

There are various ways to finish off a quilt but most of the projects in this book use a double-fold binding, which creates a firm and durable edge. Whichever edging you use a quilt will need to be squared up and trimmed first.

Making Bias Binding

The binding used to edge a quilt usually has to be pieced from several lengths. Starting with strips 2½in (6.4cm) wide, join the sections of strip with a diagonal seam. Place the end of one strip across the end of the other at right angles and sew across the overlapping part diagonally. Trim off the excess corner. Fold the complete strip in half lengthwise and press, so it's a doubled strip 1¼in (3.2cm) wide.

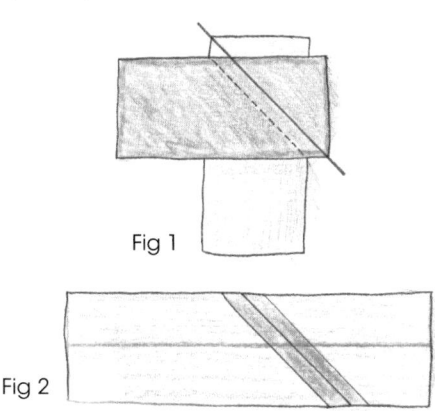

Fig 1

Fig 2

Binding

Binding is the final stage, when the raw edge of the quilt is bound with a strip of fabric sewn all around the edge. If necessary, trim the finished quilt to the desired size. A large square rule and a long ruler are helpful for this.

1 Measure the total distance all around the quilt. Cut out a strip of material 2½in (6.4cm) wide. The total length of the strip should be about 6in (15.2cm) more than the length around the quilt. If necessary the total length can be made up of several pieces (see above), and in this case allow an extra 2½in (6.4cm) total for every additional piece, to allow for the overlap between the pieces.

2 Starting part way along one side of the quilt, place the double thickness strip along the edge of the front of the quilt with the raw edges of the strip lining up with the raw edges of the quilt. Machine sew the strip to the quilt, using a walking foot if possible, ¼in (6mm) in from the edge Fig 1). Leave the first 3in (7.6cm) or so of the strip unsewn, as

you will need to join this to the other end of the strip later. As you reach each corner, stop ¼in (6mm) short of the corner and take the quilt out of the machine. Fold the strip into a mitred corner, as shown in Fig 2 and 3, and then continue sewing along the next side.

3 When you reach the beginning of the strip, trim the strip to the right length and join its two ends neatly together with a simple seam. Finish off sewing the ends of the strip to the quilt.

4 Fold the double strip over the edge of the quilt tightly all round, and hand sew its folded edge to the back of the quilt, hiding the machine stitches beneath the strip as you go (Fig 4). Fig 5 shows the mitred corner when complete.

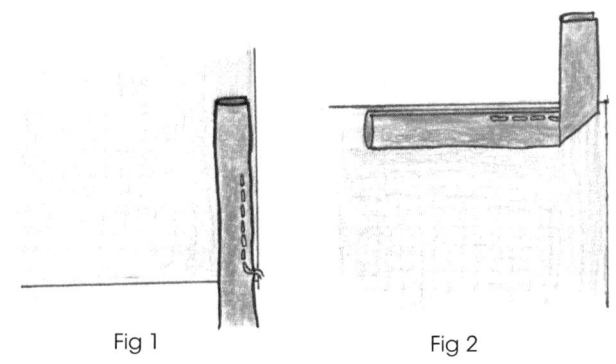

Fig 1   Fig 2

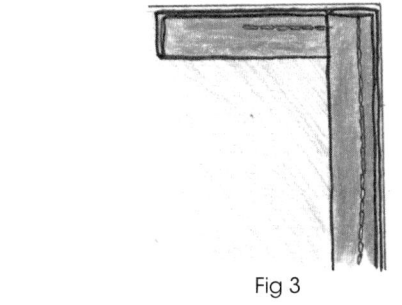

Fig 3

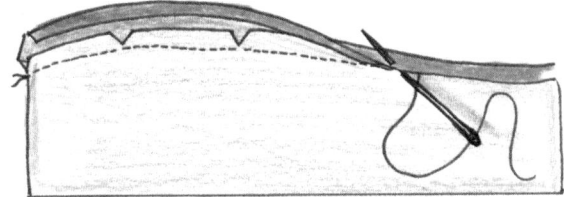

Fig 4

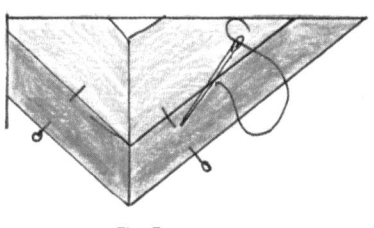

Fig 5

Templates

Using Templates

The templates are printed as seen on the finished project, which means that in some cases, depending on the technique used, it is necessary to reverse them (flip them) by tracing or on a photocopier. If reversing is needed, this is stated in the instructions, either in the relevant chapter or the Technique section.

All of the templates have been reduced to fit the book size and need to be enlarged by 250% on a photocopier to full size.

Seam allowances are ¼in (6mm) unless stated otherwise. Generally the templates show the finished size rather than the cutting line. There are exceptions but in those cases the instructions explain this. Some techniques, such as felt appliqué and machine appliqué with fusible web, need no seam allowance, so the cutting line and finished line are the same. This means that if you use a different technique from the one described you may need to adjust the fabric quantities.

For some designs with multi-part templates, such as the Basket on a Shelf Wall Hanging, it is a good idea to label all the template parts for ease of identification when using.

DRYING IN THE BREEZE
Drying in the Breeze Quilt
Templates for Panel 1
– enlarge by 250%

Templates for Panel 2 – *enlarge by 250%*

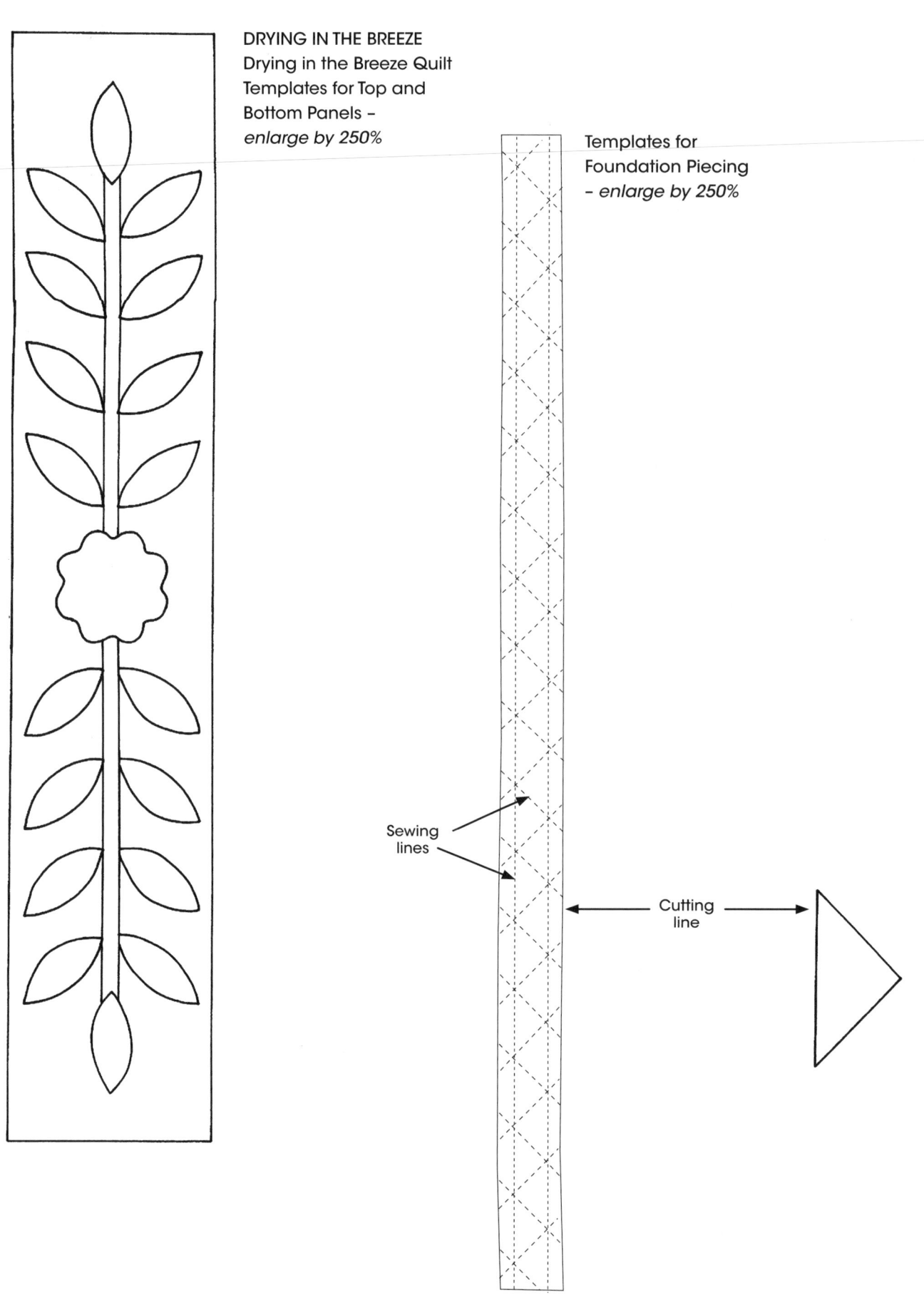

DRYING IN THE BREEZE
Drying in the Breeze Quilt
Templates for Top and
Bottom Panels –
enlarge by 250%

Templates for
Foundation Piecing
– enlarge by 250%

Sewing
lines

Cutting
line

CHRISTMAS ANGEL
Angel Doll
Templates – *enlarge by 250%*

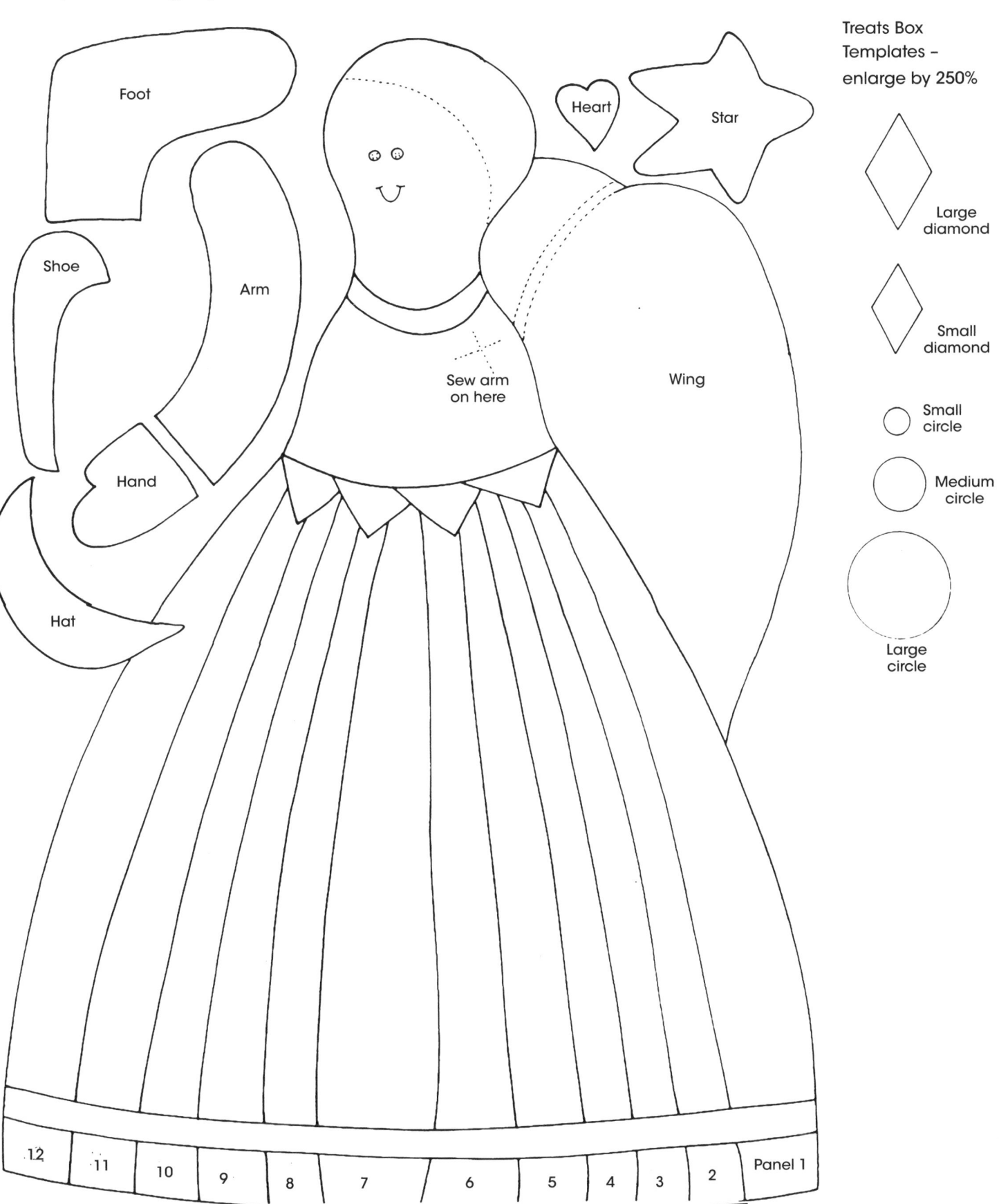

Foot

Shoe

Arm

Hand

Hat

Heart

Star

Wing

Sew arm
on here

Treats Box
Templates –
enlarge by 250%

Large
diamond

Small
diamond

Small
circle

Medium
circle

Large
circle

12   11   10   9   8   7   6   5   4   3   2   Panel 1

WOVEN BASKETS
Basket on a Shelf
Wall Hanging and
Baskets Lap Quilt
Templates (top
half, see opposite
for bottom half) –
enlarge by 250%

Handle

Basket top

Side

Warp Weft Side

Basket base

WOVEN BASKETS
Baskets Lap Quilt
Templates (quilting)
– enlarge by 250%

Leaf

Petal

WOVEN BASKETS
Basket on a Shelf Wall Hanging
and Hanging Hearts Decorations
Templates (bottom half) –
enlarge by 250%

UNDER THE GREENWOOD TREE
Birds in the Trees Pictures
Templates – *enlarge by 250%*

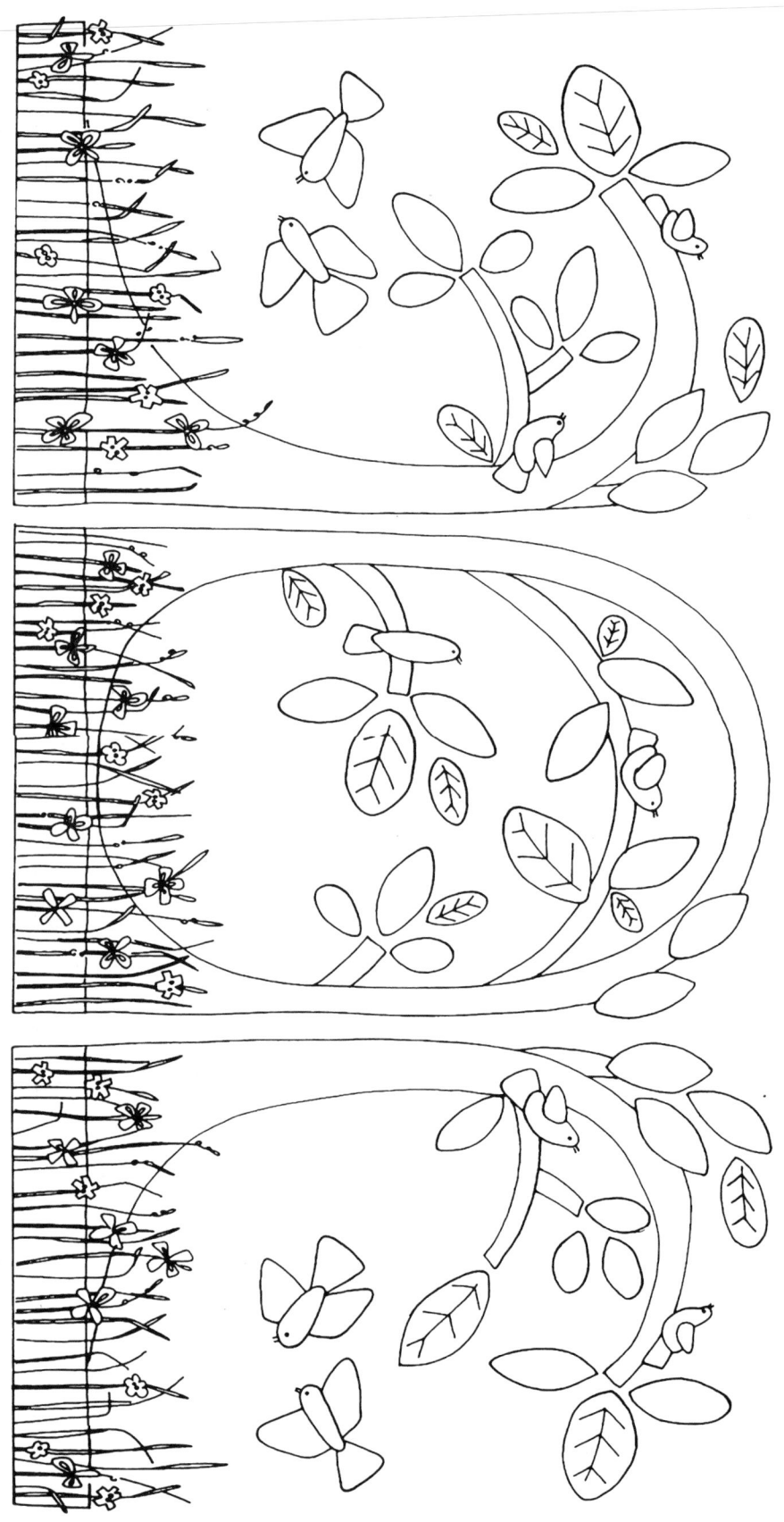

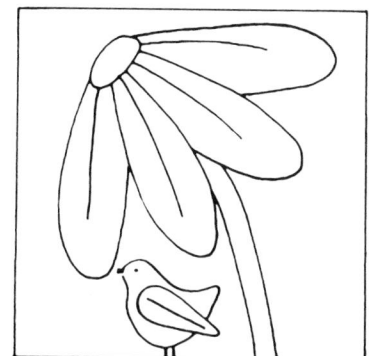

DAISY TABLE SETTING
Daisy Coaster Template
– *enlarge by 250%*

DAISY TABLE SETTING
Daisy Table Mat
Templates –
enlarge by 250%

DAISY TABLE SETTING
Daisy Table Runner
Templates (one half,
repeat for the other half)
– *enlarge by 250%*

Dashed lines indicate
quilting pattern

Little House Doorstop
Templates – *enlarge by 250%*

Chimney

Roof

Base

Roof

Chimney

LOLLIPOP FLOWERS
Flowers on the Green Quilt
Templates (foundation piecing)
– *enlarge by 250%*

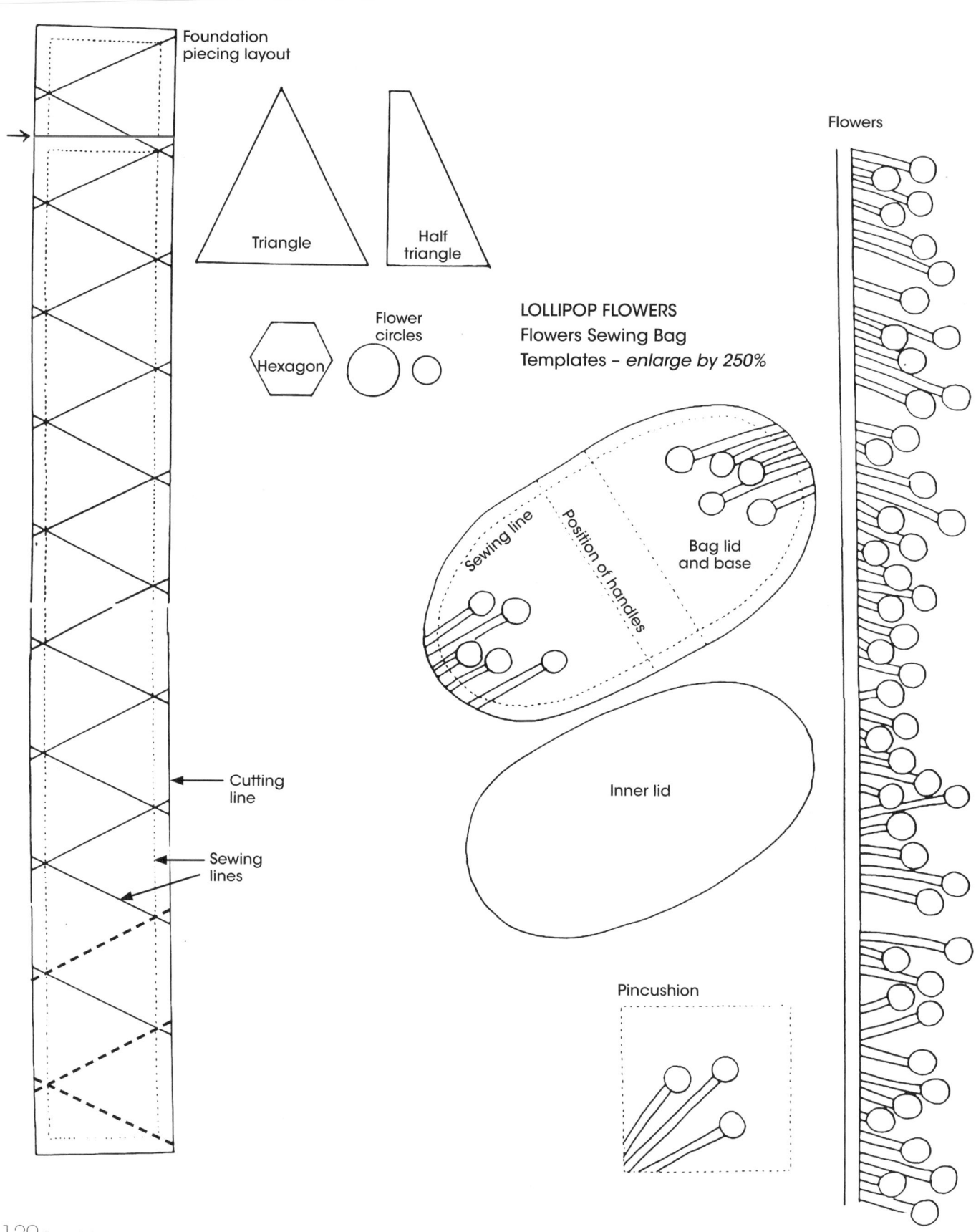

Foundation
piecing layout

Triangle

Half
triangle

Hexagon

Flower
circles

LOLLIPOP FLOWERS
Flowers Sewing Bag
Templates – *enlarge by 250%*

Flowers

Sewing line

Position of handles

Bag lid
and base

Inner lid

Cutting
line

Sewing
lines

Pincushion

ROSE BOUQUET
Rose Bag
Templates (brooch)
– enlarge by 250%

ROSE BOUQUET
Flower Button Pouch
Templates (brooch)
– enlarge by 250%

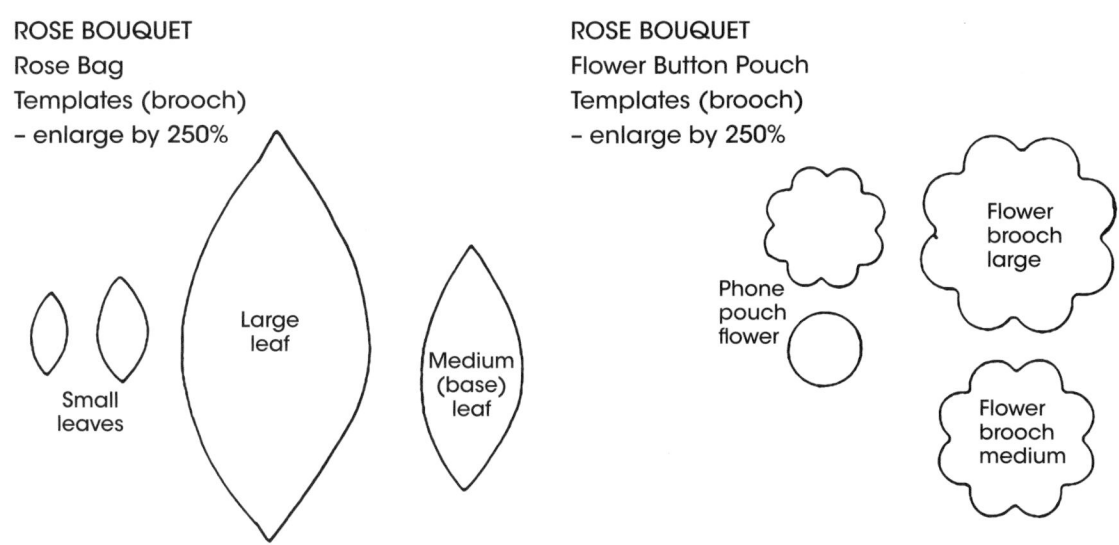

BIRDS OF A FEATHER
Feathered Friends Quilt
Template for border – enlarge by *250%*

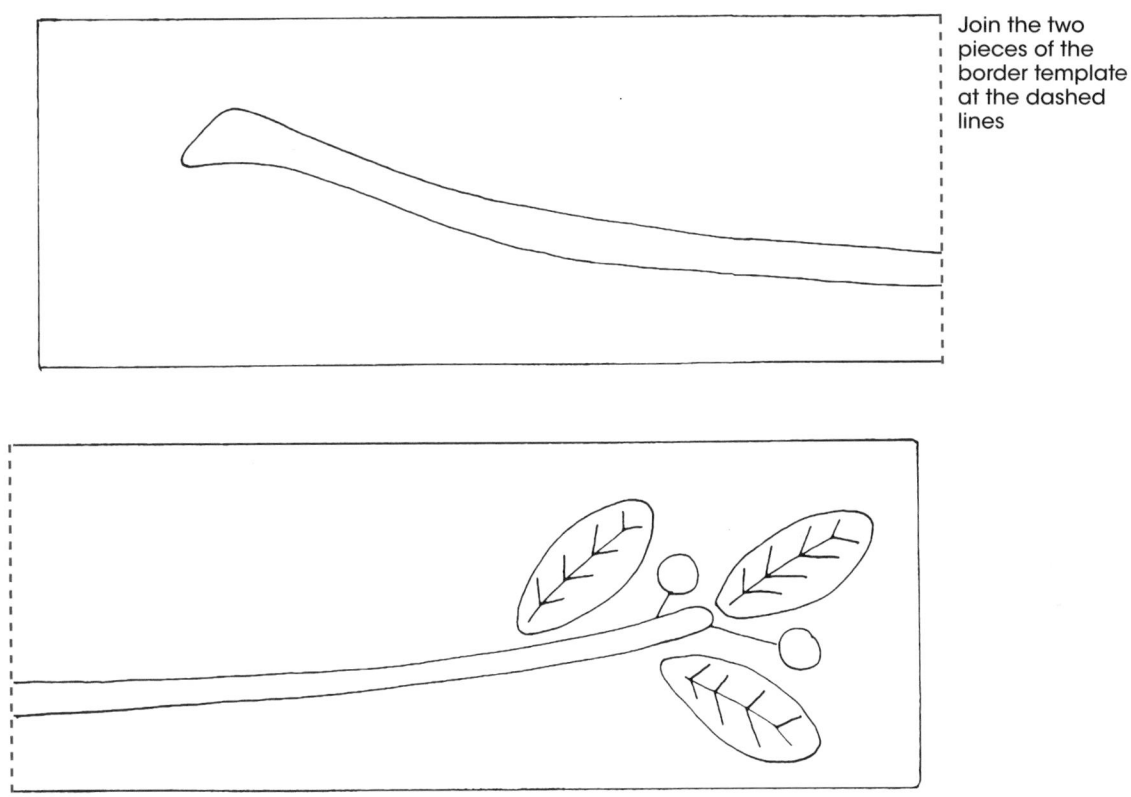

Join the two pieces of the border template at the dashed lines

BIRDS OF A FEATHER
Feathered Friends Quilt
Each block motif will be need to be reversed as well

Templates (block 1)
– *enlarge by 250%*

Templates (block 2)
– *enlarge by 250%*

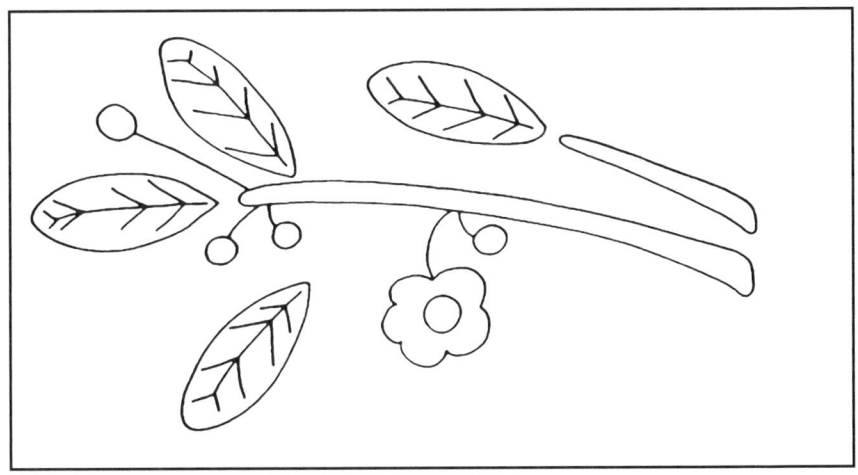

Templates (block 3)
– *enlarge by 250%*

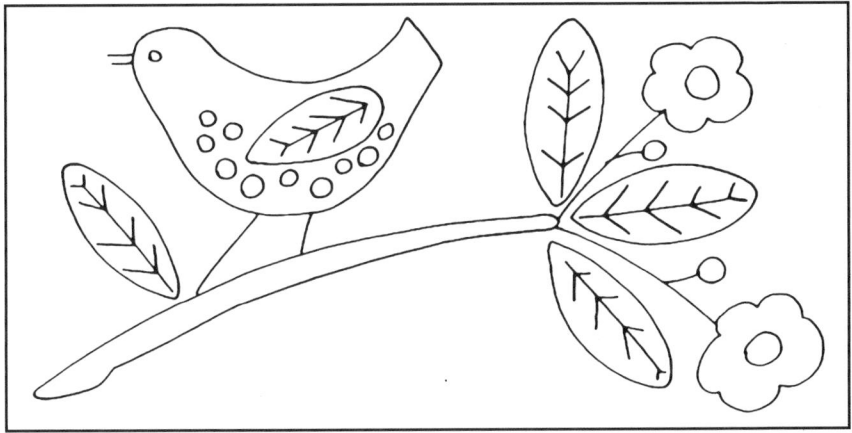

Templates (block 4)
– *enlarge by 250%*

Templates (block 5)
– *enlarge by 250%*

Templates (block 6)
– enlarge by 250%

Templates (block 7)
– enlarge by 250%

BUTTERCUP, BUTTERCUP
Buttercup Quilt
Template (border appliqué)
– enlarge by 250%

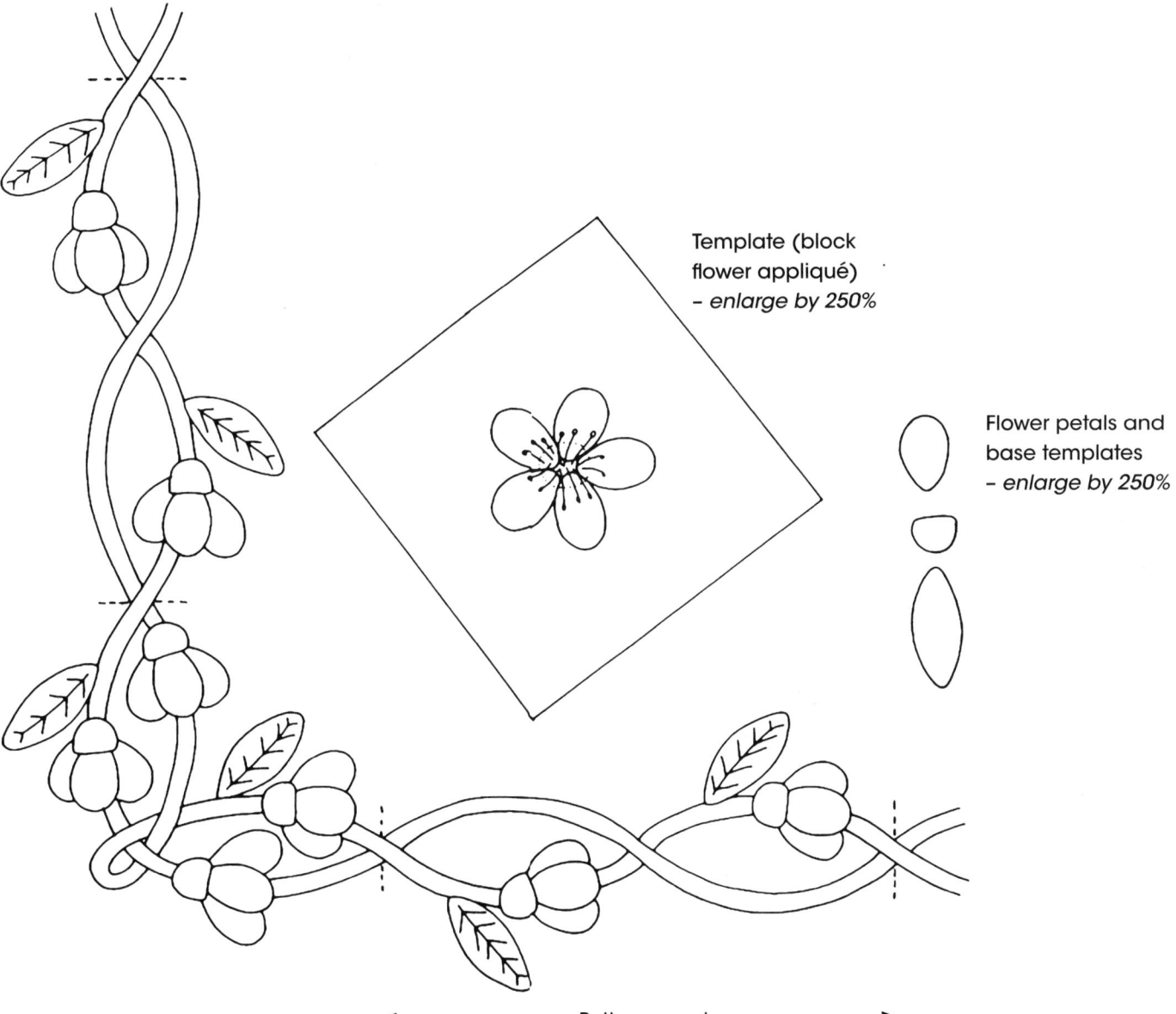

Template (block
flower appliqué)
– enlarge by 250%

Flower petals and
base templates
– enlarge by 250%

← Pattern repeat →

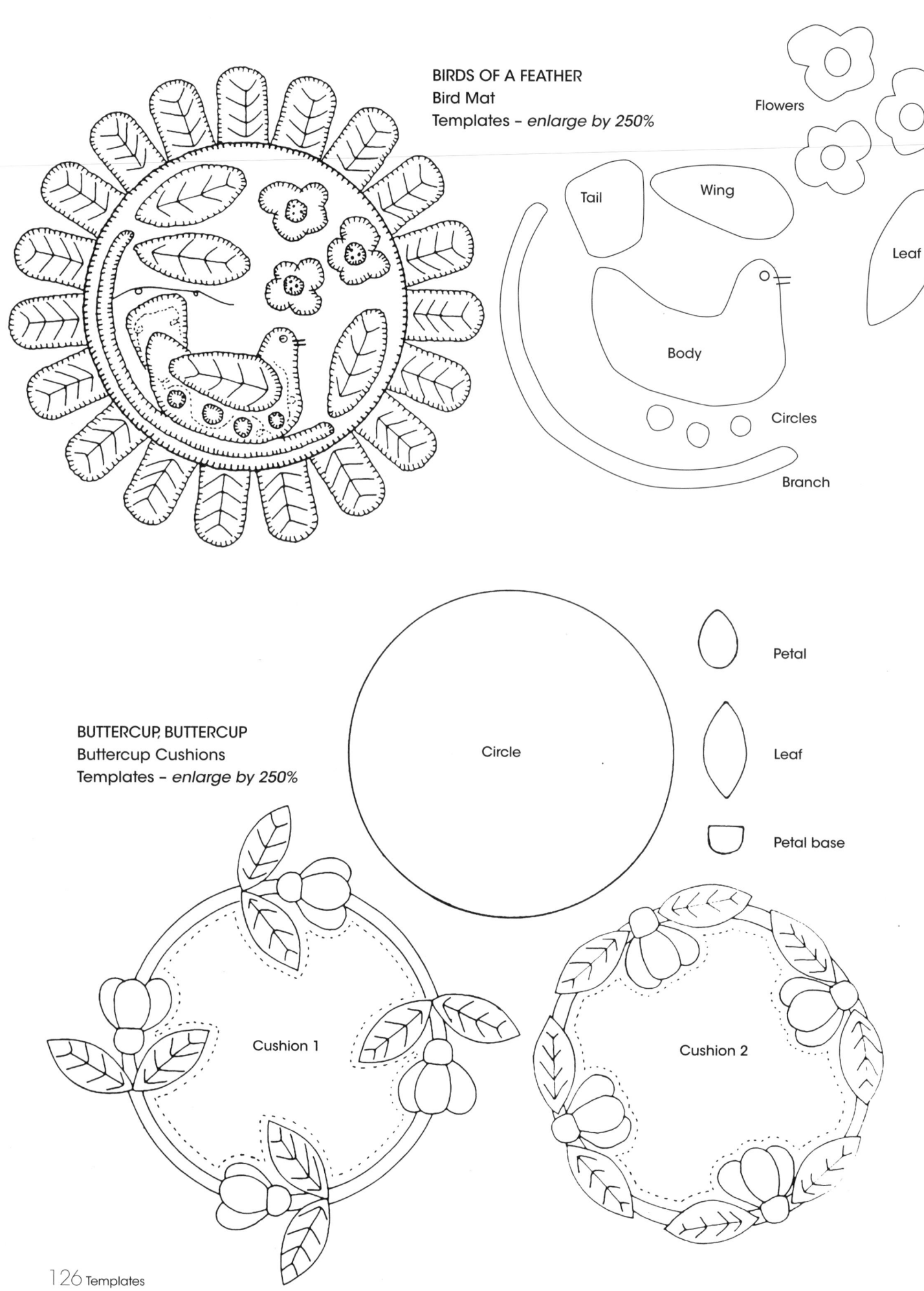

BIRDS OF A FEATHER
Bird Mat
Templates – *enlarge by 250%*

Flowers

Tail

Wing

Leaf

Body

Circles

Branch

BUTTERCUP, BUTTERCUP
Buttercup Cushions
Templates – *enlarge by 250%*

Circle

Petal

Leaf

Petal base

Cushion 1

Cushion 2

Acknowledgments

There are many people who I have to thank on my journey to here. It was Gaynor and Sandra who said that I really ought to do something with the original 'Drying in the Breeze Quilt', Jenny and later Jean who sold my patterns in their quilt shops and at the quilt shows. Liz for her tips on machine quilting, Maggie for her advice on felting. To Mo for her support and belief in me and everyone of the 'Clare's French Knots' group, you wonderful, mad lot. Thank you all. Thanks to all the team at David & Charles for their expertise in producing this book, in particular Cheryl Brown, Sarah Clark, Mia Trenoweth, Jeni Hennah and my editor, Lin Clements. I especially thank Mum for teaching me to look, my Dad and sister for their love and support, and last but not least my husband Peter, who has kept me focused these past months and has changed gobbledegook into sense.

Suppliers

UK

The Bramble Patch
West Street, Weedon, Northamptonshire, NN7 4QU
Tel: 01327 342212
www.thebramblepatch.co.uk
For fabrics and quilting supplies

The Eternal Maker
89 Oving Road, Chichester, West Sussex, PO19 7EW
Tel: 01243 788174
www.eternalmaker.com
For wool felt, haberdashery and cotton fabric

Sew and So's
14 Upper Olland Street, Bungay, Suffolk, NR35 1BG
Tel: 01986 896147
www.sewsos.co.uk
For buttons, embroidery threads and haberdashery

Village Fabrics Ltd
4–5 St Leonards Square, Wallingford, Oxfordshire, OX10 0AS
Tel: 01491 204100
www.villagefabrics.co.uk
For fabrics, wadding, buttons and haberdashery

USA

The City Quilter
133 West 25th Street, New York, NY 10001
Tel: 212 807 0390
www.cityquilter.com
For patchwork and quilting supplies

Connecting Threads
13118 NE 4th Street, Vancouver, WA 98684
Tel: 1 800 574 6454
www.connectingthreads.com
For general needlework and quilting supplies

DMC
DMC Corporation, 10 Port Kearny, South Kearny, NJ 07032-4612
Tel: (973) 589-0606
www.dmc.com
For embroidery threads and needlework supplies

Homespun Hearth
15954 Jackson Creek Pkwy, Suite B #546, Monument, CO 80132
Tel: (866) 346 0414
www.homespunhearth.com
Online shop for fabrics, wool felt and needlework supplies

About the Author

Clare Kingslake is a quilt designer and teacher specializing in appliqué techniques in a naive, country style. She is an expert in exquisite hand work and is renowned for her beautiful appliquéd quilts, bags and hangings, which have been exhibited in the UK and France. Clare's patterns are available from her website: www.clarespatterns.co.uk.

Index

back stitch 104
bag, rose 66–70, 121
baskets
    lap quilt 34–37, 114–15
    wall hanging 28–33, 114–15
bias binding, making 109
binding 109
birds
    pictures 40–45, 116
    on quilts 10, 30, 74–79,
      110, 121–24
    table mat 80–81, 126
    table setting 46, 54–55,
      117–18
blanket stitch 46, 48, 51, 54,
    74, 81, 104
border, adding 58, 76, 84, 98
box, treats 24–27, 113
brooch 66, 70, 121
buttercups
    cushions 90–93, 126
    quilt 82–89, 125
butterflies 46–50, 117–18
button, fabric 66, 73, 121

Christmas Angel 18–23, 113
circles 24–25, 38–39, 46, 56,
    74, 113
coasters, daisy 46, 117
colour 8
cushions 90–93, 126

daisies, table setting 46–50,
    54–55, 117–18
decorations, heart 38–39
doll, Christmas Angel 18–23,
    113
doorstop 46, 51–53, 119

embroidery
    hand 104–5
    machine 40, 42, 51, 76, 104
English paper piecing 24,
    58, 96
equipment 94–95

fabric 8–9, 127
felt
    appliqué 74
    needle felting 74, 95, 106
    washing 9, 76
flowers
    bird mats 80–81, 126
    brooch 66, 70, 121
    buttercups 82–93, 125, 126
    daisies 46–50
    felt 74
    lollipop 56–65, 120
    rose bag 66–70, 121
fly stitch 105

foundation piecing, triangle
    strips 12, 15, 58, 97,
    112, 120
freezer paper 95
    appliqué using 12, 20, 30,
      34, 42, 80, 90, 99–100
French knots 32, 40, 56, 86, 105
fusible web 95
    appliqué using 46, 48, 51,
      54, 76, 80, 98–99

glues 95

hand embroidery 104–5
hand sewing
    appliqué, using needle-turn
      48, 54, 102
    projects using 10, 15, 28, 40
    quilting 58, 62, 66, 68, 71,
      84, 90, 107–8
hearts 32, 38–39, 115
hexagons 59–60, 96, 120
houses 13, 46, 49–55, 110,
    117–18, 119

lazy daisy stitch 105
light box 95, 97, 102

machine 94
    appliqué 10, 12, 102
    embroidery 40, 42, 51,
      76, 104
    piecing 10, 84, 96
    quilting 20, 48, 54, 74,
      107–8
    sewing 20, 24, 40
marking fabric 94, 102
measurements 6, 9, 94

needle felting 74, 95, 106

patterned fabric 8
pictures, birds 40–45, 116
piecing
    English paper piecing
      24, 58, 96
    foundation 12, 15, 58, 97, 112
    machine 10, 84, 96
pincushion 56, 65, 120
positioning appliqué pieces 98
pouch, flower button 71–73, 121

quilting 6, 107–8
    by hand 58, 62, 66, 68, 71,
      84, 90, 107–8
    crosshatched 107
    in the ditch 108
    freehand 12, 44, 74, 108
    machine 20, 48, 54, 74,
      107–8

making a quilt sandwich
    107
    shadow 30, 33, 34, 108
quilts
    Baskets 34–37, 114–15
    Buttercup 82–89, 125
    Drying in the Breeze 10–17,
      110–12
    Feathered Friends 74–79,
      121–24
    Lollipop Flowers 56–61, 120
    mini 16–17

sashing 98
seam allowances 110
seed stitch 105
sewing bag 62–65, 120
stabilizers 95, 97, 104
stars 18, 23, 24–25, 113
stem stitch 105
stems, appliqué 42, 48,
    58, 62, 82, 87, 103
Stitch 'n' Tear 95, 97
straight stitch 105
strips
    appliquéd 12, 30, 34,
      56, 84, 90, 103
    bias-cut 10, 109
    triangle 12, 15, 58, 97,
      112, 120
    woven 28, 30
stuffed appliqué 28, 32, 34

table mats 46, 80–81, 117, 126
table runner 46–50, 118
table topper 56, 120
templates 110–26
    paper 96
    plastic 28, 38, 59, 95, 97,
      101, 102
    using 95, 101, 110
thread
    invisible 12, 95, 102
    types 95
three-dimensional shapes
    38, 66, 82, 90
tools 94–95, 104
tracing paper 95
triangle strips 12, 15, 58, 97,
    112, 120

wall hangings
    Basket on a Shelf 28–33,
      114–15
    Drying in the Breeze
      10–17, 110–12
    Lollipop Flowers 56, 120
washing 9

zip, sewing in 64–65

All techniques and templates
referred to in the book are
listed here in alphabetical
order for your reference:

Techniques
adding a border 98
appliqué using freezer
    paper 99–100
appliqué using fusible
    web 98–99
appliqué using templates
    101
appliquéd strips 103
binding 109
English paper piecing 96
foundation piecing
    triangle strips 97
hand appliqué using
    needle-turn 102
hand embroidery 104–5
machine appliqué using
    invisible thread 102
machine embroidery 104
making bias binding 109
making a quilt sandwich
    107
needle felting 106
positioning appliqué
    pieces 98
quilting 107–8
simple machine piecing
    96
using templates 110

Templates
Basket on a Shelf 114–15
Baskets Lap Quilt 114–15
Bird Mat 126
Birds in the Trees 116
Buttercup cushion 126
Buttercup quilt 125
Christmas Angel 113
Daisy Table Setting 117–18
Drying in the Breeze quilt
    110–12
Flowers Sewing Bag
Hanging Heart Decoration
    115
Little House Doorstop 119
Lollipop Flowers quilt 120
Rose Bouquet 121